RE-CREATING ME

RE-CREATING ME

MASTER THE ART OF YOUR IDENTITY

R.A. Dittmer

RACHEL ANN DITTMER

Disclaimer

Much of this book is memoir. These are memories, from my perspective, and I have tried to represent them as faithfully as possible. However, I have changed some names to protect individuals' privacy.

Copyright © 2021 Rachel Ann Dittmer

All rights reserved. No part of this book may be reproduced or used in any manner without the prior written permission of the copyright owner, except for the use of brief quotations in a book review.

To request permissions, contact the author at Rachel@lifegiver.site.

Paperback: 978-1-7376807-0-3

Edited by Brooke Bohinc
Cover art by Rachel Ann Dittmer and Allyson Morgan
Layout, artwork, and all poetry (unless otherwise stated) by Rachel Ann Dittmer

*For the woman who's lost sight of herself in
religion, marriage, or motherhood*

"You were taught, with regard to your former way of life, to put off your old self, which is being corrupted by its deceitful desires; to be made new in the attitude of your minds; and to put on the new self, created to be like God in true righteousness and holiness."
-Ephesians 4:22-24 (NIV)

So forget about who I am
See who I'm trying to be
Because who You are
Is meant to be
My identity

-from my poem *Identity*

TABLE OF CONTENTS

Preface — xi
Acknowledgments — xv
Introduction — xvii

SECTION I

Existence — 3
1. Envision — 5
2. Change Your Narrative — 15

SECTION II

Lost — 31
3. Define — 33
4. Make Room — 47
5. Stay Hungry — 57

SECTION III

Brokenness — 67
6. Fill Up — 69
7. Choose — 77
8. Return — 83
9. Commit — 97
10. Prepare Yourself — 107
11. Fight Back — 115

SECTION IV

Possibility — 125
12. Free Your Spirit — 127
13. Rest — 141
14. Know Your Worth — 151
15. Reclaim — 165
16. Take Care — 177
17. Sow — 187

SECTION V
Surrender ... 199
18. Release ... 201
19. Believe ... 211
20. Bloom ... 217

SECTION VI
Freedom ... 227
21. Dare to Live ... 229
22. Arise and Shine ... 239
23. Unite ... 251

SECTION VII
Potential ... 263
24. Collaborate ... 265
25. Change the World ... 275
26. Leave a Legacy ... 291

Conclusion ... 309
Bibliography ... 315
Index of Poetry ... 319
Notes ... 323

PREFACE

You hold in your hands a very powerful book, one I have no doubt that God led you to read. I believe it's one of many that are coming forth from women all over the world. An awakening of women that I've been witnessing, and I think has been needed for quite some time.

    I had this idea when I was in my teens that if we as women could just find out who we are and live out our potential of who God created us to be—the life givers of the next generation—we could change the world. Yet, in my attempt to live out my potential and set an example of all that a woman could be, I came to realize that all my self-righteous attempts were like filthy rags. Even after constantly striving to live up to this idea of the perfect woman within the church, I was found wanting. I had dreams of being a wife and mom, and the glorified Proverbs 31 woman because I wanted to please God with my life and heard it was the way to bring God pleasure. On the surface, I was living the life of my dreams, yet I had this deep sense of failure that I'd never be enough or that I was too much most of my life. Deep down, I was so incredibly unhappy and kept dealing with bouts of anger, bitterness, and severe depression. I felt abandoned by God, unknown and unloved in my marriage, and unseen in motherhood. At my lowest, I tried to take my life. I found I was trying to meet the different demands and expectations placed on a woman while being taught to dishonor and devalue everything that made me a woman. I didn't realize just how much I was projecting my sense of worth and value as a woman from the religious system I was entrenched in onto God.

As I followed God's leading on a journey to find health and restoration, I felt led to deconstruct all the things I had built up over my knowledge of Jesus Christ—to see with clarity all the messages that formed the blueprints of my mind and replace all the limiting beliefs that were holding me back time and again.

When I found out who I am and how much God loved me, I decided I was no longer going to allow anyone's doubts, opinions, or feelings—including my own, as well as the people and things I was conditioned to believe—to dictate my present and future anymore. I wasn't going to allow mine or other people's bad choices or disbelief to rob my life, steal my joy, or hinder my fruitfulness. I didn't need to wait around anymore for someone else to do what I thought he should for me to be who God created me to be. I decided to walk in the freedom Christ has made available and create a me that I am happy to be around. As I let go and surrendered in various areas of my life, it gave God the room to work His magic in some of the lives of those around me and brought about so much healing in my marriage and other relationships as well. It also helped release my fears that kept my spirit and creativity bound.

I want the same for you. More and more, we are finding that we can change our mindsets. Ultimately, we can recreate and alter the pathways and outcomes of our lives. As a *Living Free Ministries'* facilitator at my church, I have a heart to see people set free. I know that to do so, one must infuse life with truth and take action in walking it out.

I believe that we women are strong, capable, powerful, and resilient. Once we realize who we are, Whose we are, and why we're here, we can become co-creators in the spaces and lives of those around us rather than victims of circumstance or products of our environment, and I seek to help you do just that.

Throughout this book, you'll find my art collection titled "Woman's Revival: A Journey to Wholeness" as well as various poems I've written along my journey. I hope they help bridge the gap from where you are and give you a vision to where you're going so you can show up in life and live up to your God-given potential.

See you on the other side,
-R.A.D.

ACKNOWLEDGMENTS

Drew, thank you for wanting to do life with me, partnering with me on this crazy roller coaster of a journey we've been on, and for taking over at times when I needed to get away and write. I needed to hear that others could benefit from hearing my and our story and that I had something worthwhile to say. Thank you.

Kids - AnnaBella (Bella), Austin, Madelyn (Maddie), Jesse, and Sophie - I hope this inspires you to not give up on your dreams like I'm not giving up on mine. I can't wait to see all of your stories unfold and how God chooses to use you and speak through you. I'm so grateful for you all and all your fierce personalities—most of the time at least. ;) God's never afraid to work through your messes even when your parents struggle to. I love you no matter what.

Becky, thank you for always believing in me and speaking God's truth over my life. I don't want to know where I'd be without you, sista.

David Jones, ask and you shall receive. Haha. Love you, big brotha. You too, Cathy and Josh, Dad and Mom. Thank you for putting up with me all these years and showing you love me some of the time too. ;) I'm so grateful for you all.

Anna Winzeler, thank you for being a lifelong friend to me, and all you Winzelers for being like family to me. My childhood wouldn't have been nearly as sweet without you all.

Julie Bialek, thank you for extending so much grace and kindness to me when I was at my worst. I can't imagine where I'd be without your friendship in the season I needed you most. You're such a blessing!

Tanya Klimchuk, thank you for believing in me, encouraging this book, and helping me move forward in so many ways. I'm so thankful for your wisdom in my life and helping me embrace everything that comes with being a woman.

Kim Dzula (Mrs. Dzula to me), thank you for your dedication to us students and staying behind to teach me and others how to read so long ago. You sparked a love for reading, learning, and teaching in my life that never died out. I'm forever grateful for you!

Thank you to my closest childhood friends that made my life so much more enjoyable- Debby, Elaina, Grace, Jenn, Leticia, and all you Brunzes. You all are gems. I'm so thankful for you!

I had to save the best for last. God, I don't know what I'd do without You. Thank You for not giving up on me and considering me worthy of all You've called me to. I'm praying You use this to touch whoever needs it and use my mess to bring You glory like only You can.

INTRODUCTION

It was late fall of 2007 when I downed enough aspirin to end my life prematurely. All my dreams and aspirations, everything I longed for in life, no longer seemed possible. I felt stuck. The very foundations I built my whole life upon seemed to be crumbling underneath my feet, and I was at a loss on how to stop it. I no longer felt safe and loved. I no longer felt capable of living in freedom. It was as though I forgot how to live life entirely, and suicide seemed to be the best option.

Around everyone else, I was smiling, laughing even. Not many people would have suspected it. In truth, not many people were really even close enough to me at the time to have noticed the change in the atmosphere. Those who were closest in proximity to me knew so little about me. Those who did chime in on my life seemed to want me to fall in line with them and gave advice with little to no true information. My environment was toxic and so were the people around me. My circumstances led me to feel like a victim in life. Even worse, I stopped believing that God cared for me, so I had no one I trusted that I felt I could turn to. My life became a living hell.

Bitterness and unforgiveness became a powerful stronghold in my life. They entangled every fiber of my being and were choking the life out of me. My dreams became living nightmares as I felt justified to hold onto them. It seemed like I couldn't escape. Years before, I prayed that God would do whatever it took for me to get closer to Him and become who I was meant to be in order to be used for His glory. Let's just say that's a very bold prayer to pray, and God wants to answer it. That answering of prayer will look different for every person depending on one's own personal story, but the process I've found to be very similar as well as the rebuilding of one's life and identity.

This book is about that process. One of my favorite things in life as an artist is to take those worn out, tired, forgotten, and beaten-up things and bring them back to life.

I've found that at some point or another we all have or will feel like we've lost our way. We all wonder if our lives are too much of a mess or our hopes and dreams too far gone to do anything with them. We all long for the "good old days" and wish we could have a do-over where we would right all those wrongs we've made.

What if I told you that the mess you're in and those weaknesses you have are the medium God wishes to use to paint His most beautiful masterpieces? What if I told you that those unfortunate circumstances and toxic environment you're in are the very soil in which God wishes to grow you? You may feel like there's no hope for you or your story. You may wish for a spiritual amnesia to move past your unforgiveness like I did. You may want to go back in time and tell your younger self the lessons you've learned and the wisdom you've gained with age and experience.

This book was written to help you right where you're at. You don't need to go back in time. You don't need to right your wrongs. You aren't too far gone that God can't use you. I have so much hope for you because I've been right where you are, and God has been helping me rebuild and renew my life one day at a time. Let me share with you those things God has been teaching me along the way and the hope He's given me. I know the best is yet to come for both of us!

SECTION I

1

ENVISION

"Where there is no vision, the people perish."
Proverbs 29:18a (KJV)

Then the Lord answered me and said:
"Write the vision
And make *it* plain on tablets,
That he may run who reads it.
For the vision *is* yet for an appointed time;
But at the end it will speak, and it will not lie."
Habakkuk 2:2-3a (NKJV)

"Do you feel stupid for what you did?" the doctor condescendingly asked me when he came into my emergency room before dismissal. The only stupidity I felt at the time was for not coming up with something quicker, more permanent, and with less side effects. I had to drink a cup full of charcoal; and for three days, my body did everything it could to get rid of the poison I swallowed in order to end my life. However, my life felt hopeless long before this incident. I sat there staring at the blank white walls feeling utterly numb and empty as I listened to the doctor's attempt at shaming me for my choice and started picturing a painting I had done only a couple months before—a girl soaking in the rain. That girl in the painting was meant to be me, but I wasn't even close to being able to fully picture myself in that stage of life. This vision of myself where I could let go of everything, soak in "the rain," and truly be free. As I sat there picturing that and feeling everything I felt, I knew I wasn't the first who sat in this place and wouldn't be the last. I couldn't imagine feeling the way I felt without such a vision and knew that I wanted to do everything I could to make my vision a reality, for myself and others.

I WAS in a high school English and Literature class reading *The Canterbury Tales* when our teacher asked us to write our own epitaph. We were challenged to think about how we wanted to be remembered and what we would want people to say about us at the end of our lives. This was what I wrote:

UNEARTHED TREASURE

I was a young girl looking for meaning in life,
Always wanting more than this world could offer.
Always searching, always seeking;
My soul would never find rest.
Every once in a while, I'd stumble upon a joyful soul
With a twinkle in merry-filled eyes,

And knew they must have been one of the few
to find this hidden Treasure.
Oh, how I wanted to be one of these few.
I wanted to explore and discover the vastness of It.
I would cherish every piece of this sacred Gift,
For I acknowledged many sorrow-filled souls
have never unearthed It.
I sought day and night; and in despair,
Apprehension told me I couldn't find It on my own.
In my desperation, I uttered a downcast plea,
for no ear to receive.
And to my astonishment, Purpose came seeking
to find a home in my heart.
I found Him that day, the Meaning of my life,
And have shared Him with many-a-weary souls
who have sought just as I.
Now, I'm spending eternity with this Treasure,
And my soul can now find rest.

"Ask, and it will be given to you; seek, and you will find; knock,
and it will be opened to you. For everyone who asks receives,
and he who seeks finds, and to him
who knocks it will be opened."
Matthew 7:7-8 (NKJV)

"For where your treasure is, there
your heart will be also."
Matthew 6:21

IT WAS that vision that saved me from giving into a lot of peer pressure growing up. It was vision that has helped me develop a lot of self-control and form good habits even when it was so tempting to give up. It is vision for the different houses we've renovated that has helped me see them through until the end. It was vision for the joy of seeing our babies and trying to do what's best for them that helped me naturally endure the pain of six labors and five childbirths. It was the vision for the joy set before Jesus that helped Him endure the cross.[1]

Vision gives pain purpose and helps one develop self-control and discipline. Without vision, people lack purpose and cast off restraint.[2]

It is so good to have a vision for your life. We're told to write down our vision, and I believe we should. If we don't know what we want out of life or the direction we want to go, how will we know what steps to take? We'll wander around confused or be easily swayed to live a self-indulgent life without meaning or purpose. I wrote a poem about it in high school:

THE WAY IS YOU

What am I supposed to do?
Where am I supposed to go?
Are there really "supposed-tos?"
I'd really like to know

I'm hidden in a crowd
And I'd like to know my way
I'm going around in circles
That I walked just yesterday

But I saw all the same people
They took the same route as I

Am I the only one lost?
Are we all following blind?

I stopped to ask the woman
Who was next to me
If she could be anywhere
Where would it be?

She looked confused
All battered and bruised
The scars I saw upon her soul
She wondered if you
Could even choose
Which way you would go

We're not stuck in quicksand
We're not even blind
We don't have a dictator
Only limited time

And the experiences we encounter
Always consume our mind
And we've closed off truth
To listen to Satan's lies

And if only one person
Could find that Jesus is the way
Wouldn't be consumed
With religious play

If only one person
Gave up his rights
Gave up self-attempts
Let God shine His light

We would all be led
To live a life beyond ourselves
With purpose, direction
Lives without question

Of whether we lived in vain
Because if people opened their eyes to see
They'd find truth lies in Jesus
Not you and me

But we all keep following the crowd
Of pointing to ourselves
Our self-attempts at religiosity
And I wonder if we
Ever stopped to think
We're leading others to our own personal hell

Where would we all be?
If we ever stopped to love Jesus
And others more than ourselves
If we stopped to let Jesus in us
To work through us
And let Him be the light

Instead of dimming His truth
And following blindly in the dark
Or showing half-truths
Because we're afraid of the stark contrast
We might be among the crowd

When all we want is the light
The purpose, the Truth
To stop hiding because of shame
And we all want to know His name

But we're too afraid
To say it

Jesus, Jesus, be our light
Be our Guide
Through this thick darkness
That covers the night
Help us find our way back to You
Uncover the truth
That the way is You

I CLEARLY KNEW THE WAY, the Truth, and the Life even at a "young" age. I had a vision for my life. I lived with purpose and meaning and said "yes" to God so completely that everything else paled in comparison. I wanted to be used by God however He saw fit. I wanted to live in a beautiful, surrendered way that helped others.

My vision for my life wasn't a bad one. If anything, it was actually good. It was an image of perfection. No, really—my vision involved me doing everything right, not messing up or making any mistakes, and being an example for others to follow because I had discovered the meaning to life and knew Who to turn to and Who to allow to direct my path. I seemed to think that if I followed God with my life from an early age, that meant I wouldn't stumble. If I lived a life of purity and saved my first kiss and so many firsts for my husband, if I became this Proverbs 31 woman that everyone spoke so highly about and became a helpmeet for my husband and sought to make myself ideal marriage material, then our marriage would be glorious. If we righted all the wrongs of our parents' mistakes and parented perfectly, we would have well-behaved children who would also live a pain-free, purposeful life. I mean, we'd have depth just because God did, and we'd be following Him. There wouldn't be pain, miscarriage, marriage troubles, dishonesty or infidelity, abuse, disobedience, stumbling, or setbacks. I know—reading that now seems hilarious. God probably thought it was too.

My vision didn't include pitfalls, screw-ups, or messes. It didn't involve any clean up at all. It didn't need to be renewed. I had many plans that seemed so right, that led to my death figuratively speaking.[3] While my vision was short-sighted and naive —completely seen in black and white—it came from a pure heart wanting to do what was right. My visions weren't what needed to be corrected so much as the process and journey it took to get there. I learned that not only did I have a vision for my life, but so did God and Satan. Satan wanted to use my setbacks to get me to a place where he could steal, kill, and destroy my life and the vision God had for me. God wanted to use my setbacks to bring me to a place of surrender. My journey needed to be disrupted or else I would have thought it was somehow my dreams, plans, and actions that led me to my freedom. I didn't know what to do when the vision I had for my life fell short, but God did. I felt stuck as so many others do, while God was patiently waiting for me to allow Him to take over. I thought I was powerful enough to ruin God's plan for my life— the God who started a work in me, saw the end from the beginning, knew about it before time began, and had already factored my ignorance in when He promised to finish the work He started. Thankfully, He's in the business of restoration. God has a lot of practice bringing dead things back to life. Even better, our weakness is the very substance He wishes to use to reveal His strength.[4] His most creative masterpieces come from the biggest fixer uppers.

I've found that my vision, while good, was so incredibly limited. My view and understanding of God were restricted to the experiences I and others had, which were few and distorted at times. I had a lot of head knowledge from hearing and reading God's Word my entire life, but so many truths had yet to sink into my heart. His depth and wisdom are so vast that we can only handle so much at a time. Through His infinite love, He spares us from carrying some of the heavier things until we can lift them with His help. Clearly, in my finite mind, I am nowhere near to holding the supernatural wisdom, truths, and blessings God has for us. I cannot ever fully understand or possibly even grasp the vision He has planned for my life. Even when He does give me a glimpse, it always ends up differently than the scenario I've created in my head. His view is not limited like mine is. His plans are far above any I could ever come up with and extend much further.

Reflect:

WHAT IS the vision you have for your life? What do you want it to look like? What is it you dream of doing or being?

WHATEVER YOUR VISION, I'd encourage you to pray about it and write it down. You won't know what steps to take to get from where you are now to where you want to go if you don't.

WHEN THINGS HAPPEN in life beyond your control or understanding that seem unfair and unjust, you might need to shift your perspective a bit further and change your narrative.

2

CHANGE YOUR NARRATIVE

"What if everything in your life, including the most painful and traumatic events, was happening for you, not to you?"
Tony Robbins

"But Joseph said to them, 'Don't be afraid.
Am I in the place of God?
You intended to harm me, but God intended it for good to accomplish what is now being done,
the saving of many lives.'"
Genesis 50:19-20 (NIV)

"*Look* Mom, Jesus healed me!" I was four. Earlier that day, I was playing with two neighborhood friends, both boys around my age. We were going down the slide different ways. When I asked one to scoot back so I could go down another way, he grew tired of waiting and pushed me off, causing my collarbone to break. Like most kids, I had a habit of being overly dramatic with my injuries. My dad thought I was probably being a baby like usual, and in an effort to see if it was really broken, he moved it. Of course, I screamed and was taken to the doctor after that. The doctor told me it was broken in such a way that he wasn't sure if it would ever fully heal.

My mom went to a church she regularly visited in addition to our own church that night called "Word Alive" with me as her tagalong like normal. That night, they showed R.W. Shambach talking about his early days, training as a minister under A.A. Allen, where God did an extremely awesome miracle for a little boy born with several major handicaps including his feet turned backwards among other things. While A.A. Allen and the congregation prayed, the little boy's feet were corrected, and he was completely healed of every ailment and handicap he had. I had to ask my mom for those specific details since it was so long ago. However, I remember seeing the video and vividly thinking in my head how if God could heal that little boy so completely of all his deformities, then surely, He could heal my arm. Almost immediately upon thinking that, as I was only listening and watching beside my mom without anyone praying over me even, I felt my collarbone being healed. I raised my arms and excitedly proclaimed, "Look mom, Jesus healed me!" With what happened and my mom's reaction, the entire congregation gathered around me, praising God for His miraculous power that was shown through His healing of my arm.

From that moment on, I knew that God was alive and real. I knew He was there and listening. Better yet, I knew He cared about me. I saw God's capabilities and His heart towards me by the fact that He answered my little heart's desire in healing my arm without me even saying it out loud. That formed such a blueprint in my mind. It was the foundation—the "good bones" that every other thing in my life was built upon. I remember so many nights hugging and kissing the air in response to those thoughts knowing that God could hear them and feel my love for Him as He had the night He healed my arm.

My parents had a small group that met at their house during that time where my mom would play the piano as everyone sang. My favorite song at the time was a song that said, "Sing unto the Lord a new song, sing unto the Lord all the earth." I danced, sang, and twirled around the living room in joyous response and confidence of how I felt about God. At the time, I didn't care what others thought about my display. I felt loved, was in love, and didn't care who knew it.

In my teens, I wrote about my experience in a poem:

A CHILD'S LOVE

Apathy seems to be taking over
Logical thinking seems to define me now
But deep underneath, I miss the passion
Without the knowledge trying to define expressions how

I miss the free flowing, passion-driven
Child-like spirit, which used to drive me
The kisses and hugs to an invisible Love
That only I could see

I miss the days You felt so near
In the midst of heartache and pain
Giving of my all to You
Knowing I had everything to gain

And the selfless acts a child would make
To express everything her heart knew
For no one need ever explain

How to love You

For love needs no definition
Needs no dictionary to explain how to
For when one heart feels Love
You must know I love You

This knowledge I claimed was never mine
And this apathy it gave is slipping away
I'm going back to what I knew to be true
For a child's love means forever and a day

And I'll always remain Your loving child
Embracing the Love I know to be true
And this untamed heart will remain wild
To express just how much I love You

W‍HEN I WAS SIXTEEN, I had one of the worst months of my entire life. My best friend and sister moved out of state. My brother moved out a couple days later, and I was forbidden to hang out with him for a while, so it felt like I lost two siblings within days of each other. My favorite grandma died. My cousin was in a car accident and became paralyzed, and while my aunt was visiting her son, her uncle died in the same hospital. Before the month was over, I was supposed to help lead a small group during our youth group camp, and I was a mess. I was surrounded by people, friends even, yet I felt lonelier than ever. It didn't feel like anybody could relate. I wrote a poem during one of those first nights at camp that seemed to set the stage for the next season of my life:

CONQUERING LONELINESS

Loneliness sets in
Creeping within
This emptiness in my heart
Is tearing me apart
I just want to run away from all of this
As loneliness smirks and gives me a kiss
Satan feels as though he has defeated, conquered all
Feels as though he's made me fall
But that's not true at all
All it's made me do is break the barrier, break the wall
Hear His voice, and listen to His call
He's calling me
He's gonna set me free
From all this loneliness that's inside of me

MY EXPERIENCES SET a new precedent in my life. Rather than turning to other people or things when I experienced loneliness or heartache, I turned solely to God. Rather than listening to my thoughts, I used my thoughts to speak to God. When bad things happened in my life, I went to Him. When good things happened, I started thanking Him. I started journaling to God and writing more poetry than ever. God started answering prayers I never told a soul. He was answering even the simple desires of my heart. When I didn't have time to pack a meal for work as a garage cashier after school, five people would randomly tip one dollar each or someone would drop off a meal without me asking. When my sister who lived far away talked about coming to my graduation but would need to fly in order to make it happen, I asked if I paid half the plane ticket if she could match it and come. Around that same time, a lady from another state who started reading my blog said she and her husband were praying and felt like they were supposed to give their tithes to me, which ended up being the exact amount I needed. Situations like these started becoming a regular occurrence. They reminded me that God was as real as He was when I was a child and He cared enough to listen to the prayers of my heart.

Over time, I wanted nothing more than to share the same hope God had given me with others. I prayed that God would use me to remind others of His goodness just like He used the people in my life. Often, the smaller the thing, the more I knew He cared, so I knew that God could use even small things too. It helped take the pressure off of feeling like my contributions would be insignificant.

As my heart for God and others grew, so did my prayers. Over time, I didn't even realize the fact that I stopped questioning whether God was speaking back to me through my thoughts. It just felt like we were in tune with each other. My needs weren't the only needs being met, but those needs I prayed for over others were met too. I often felt like I could sense what other people were struggling with or going through, and I was able to give them a word of knowledge or just encourage them with God's promises I had read in His word. Many times, people would ask me how I knew those things about them they never shared with me or tell me I had wisdom beyond my years or that I told them exactly what they needed to hear. My only understanding was that God knew and cared and my thoughts were in line with His. While life circumstances definitely weren't easy for me then, the joy of the Lord was my strength, and I knew I could trust Him with my life.

At the time, it didn't feel like there was any possible way that I could get closer to God, yet I knew there was so much more I must be missing out on. Through every trial I'd gone through, I got closer to God as He had reestablished the fact that He is good and that I could trust Him through it all. Those experiences left me feeling somewhat invincible in a way. I felt like no matter what would or could come my way, I would remain faithful to God. In that mindset, I prayed that He would do whatever it took to bring me closer to Him and to use me however He wanted in other people's lives. My biggest desire was to be the person God created me to be and be used however He saw fit. He was my Creator, and I trusted that He knew what was best for me and that He would see me through whatever came my way.

LET'S just say that over the course of the next decade, God answered my prayers. He didn't answer them at all in the way that I thought He would. In fact, it was as though God led me into the biggest wilderness season of my entire life. Every plan I made was disrupted. In every close relationship I had, I experienced heartache and pain to the point where I couldn't trust anyone. I was lied to, falsely accused, bullied, cheated on, anger was taken out on me, and/or I was just neglected by different people in my life among other things. There wasn't one person I felt I could rely on anymore. My health took a sharp turn for the worse, and my mentality was hit hard time and again. The only people who did speak into my life knew so little about me and only went by the little or false information they had heard. I tried turning to God through it all, but He seemed utterly absent. I had never experienced so much emptiness even to this day. Originally, I was proud of how I handled the situations I encountered. It seemed like certain obstacles were so obviously the enemy's effort to throw me off course, yet I remained faithful to God through it all. I still sought Him. I still prayed and tried to love those people who seemed like they hated me. I was still so sure that God would be right around the corner to give me some relief and I would reap the benefits of these trials. Yet, year after year, all I felt was absence. All my prayers seemed to be met with silence. All my plans, dreams, and everything I thought I had done right over the course of my life was used against me. My reputation and character were slandered, and I was unloved and rejected.

I never once stopped believing in God through it all. I had seen and experienced too much of Him in my lifetime to ever deny His existence. Yet, somewhere along the way through the course of all my trials, I stopped thinking that God cared about me. Like the people in Malachi 3, I started wondering what the benefits were for following Him and keeping His commands. I started looking on with jealousy at those people who seemed to walk through life so carelessly because I didn't feel free to be careless like them. My upbringing and beliefs were so set on doing everything I knew to be right, while others didn't seem to care how their actions affected themselves or others and used those things to their benefit. Worse yet, I saw that so many seemed utterly loved—mistakes, purposeful wrong actions, and all. Yet here I was, doing everything "right," and I felt so unloved. In the past, I would have looked on those who were stuck in some sort of sin in love, thinking they were missing out on God's goodness in some way. Even still, I knew deep down that I wanted everyone to be loved completely—flaws and all—by God and others. However, when I didn't feel like God or anyone else around me loved me no matter what I did, those same things I would have looked on with pity and love now seemed to be a reason for jealousy and self-pity. My love began to grow cold towards God and others.

In an effort to protect myself, I built up these invisible walls around my heart where I didn't allow anything to come in or flow out freely anymore. I did all the "right" actions, yet I lost my softness in the process. Rather than serving God out of the knowledge that I was loved and in love, I started serving Him in an effort to earn His love. All those things that once seemed so easy to me started feeling like mountains to overcome or crosses to bear. The gospel no longer seemed like good news anymore; it felt more like slavery. I hated that I couldn't shake God or His existence out of my life because I still feared Him, yet I didn't feel loved by Him. All those promises that you'll reap what you sow seemed entirely lost on me. I wasn't reaping what I sowed, and I didn't know why I couldn't stop caring about God or what He thought. I could no longer envision Heaven anymore. While I was terrified of dying and going to Hell in such a state, my life was already a living hell that I felt I had no hope for escape.

When I tried to take my life, I was done. It wasn't a cry for attention or help. I don't like being pitied or labeled. My parents didn't even find out until twelve years after the fact, and unless people have read or heard some of my testimony, they wouldn't know at all. Before that time, God was the One being I felt I could rely on, yet I didn't feel like I could count on Him anymore either.

AT THE BEGINNING OF 2014, God gave me a different narrative. I was in the middle of a blog post, writing something so seemingly unrelated to the subject at the time, when I felt led to share some of my story. As I started, I felt like God was calling me to fast from food until I was done. I had the feeling that sharing my story was going to be much bigger than what I'd had in mind. I didn't quite understand what that meant, but although it had been so long since I was sure God was speaking to me, I knew I wouldn't have thought to fast on my own. I had just finished reading through the New Testament again the night before, and I was drawn to the fact that Jesus seemed to be moved with compassion every single time before a miracle happened. The only time His disciples couldn't perform a miracle was due to the fact that the demonic strongholds they were up against had to be conquered through fasting and prayer.[1] As I fasted and prayed and started sharing my testimony, it was as though I was able to walk through everything I had gone through in my life all over again. Only this time, it wasn't from the perspective I had—it was from God's perspective.

From His perspective, every single traumatic event in my life was because God chose me from before the foundations of this world to be His,[2] and it put a target on me from our enemy.[3] Every single lie or false accusation that people spoke over me[4] in a place of judgement was because Satan wanted to use those closest to me to set me off course. It wouldn't have had the same impact if it was people whose opinions I didn't care about. He showed me how those same people were hurting and in bondage as well, and that He had every desire to free them.[5] All these situations I had gone through were because Satan wanted to harm me and others. Yet God wanted to use my story to help set others free just like in the story of Joseph when Joseph told his brothers who put him in exile this: "Don't be afraid. Am I in the place of God? You intended to harm me, but God intended it for good to accomplish what is now being done, the saving of many lives."[6]

God gave me this hope that if I could conquer this mountain and learn to love those who seemed so unlovable and toxic in my life, then there was hope for anyone. He was going to use what I had gone through to help others walk in freedom.[7] I felt too far gone, so powerless, and stuck, but God showed me that He started a work in my life and was going to complete it.[8] He hadn't left me and was there every step of the way—even those times I felt so utterly alone.[9] Better yet, God showed me that He overwhelmingly loved me in my mess—exactly where I was.[10] He didn't love me more only when I was in tune with Him, but He loved me right then as I was.[11] He didn't expect perfection out of me like I had.[12] God wanted to work with my mess and create a masterpiece.[13] I didn't screw up His plans for my life. From God's point of view, I was so small in comparison and His plans and thoughts were much higher than my own.[14] God saw a much bigger picture than I possibly could. He already knew the end from the beginning,[15] and He had already factored in my weaknesses, mistakes, detours, and sins—using them for my good and to bring about His glory[16] because I loved Him and was called according to His purpose.[17]

I went into fasting in the mindset that I had every right to be angry and unforgiving and wondering why things happened to me, but I came out of it feeling honored that God chose me,[18] and that He loved me enough to allow me to go through everything I had to help others. I felt more loved than I had ever felt in my entire life and wanted so badly to share His love and hope with others. Some days it would take half a day to an entire day to write one blog post, yet I had written forty-eight pages worth during my time of fasting. Things that seemed too good to be true[19] and verses that I didn't know I had tucked in the back of my mind jumped at me with incomprehensible clarity. I wept for an entire day. It wasn't out of anger and sadness anymore though but pure joy.[20] My husband didn't understand it at the time, and I didn't fully understand it either. All I knew was that I didn't even know such an experience was available to us. If I wasn't solely reading the New Testament at the time[21] and didn't see the fruits that came from it,[22] it would have terrified me even more than it had after the fact. The softening of my heart towards my husband and others who had hurt me helped both of us to never doubt it was God's doing.

When God changed the narrative of my story, I was the happiest I had ever been up to that point. Everything seemed entirely possible.[23] God's plans seemed too good to be true. Nothing seemed too hard for Him.[24] His goodness overwhelmed me and caused me to repent of my self-pity, unforgiveness, and bitterness.[25] God got my entire focus off of myself and my hardships and onto what He could do through me for others.[26] As I was reminded of His goodness and benefits, I had this hope that the best was yet to come.[27] I saw how much He cared about me and others and how faithful He was even when I was unfaithful.[28] It was the refreshing my soul needed[29] before I was going to go through yet another stormy season when God allowed me to go through some more testing.[30] I thought from there on out things would get easier again. It was only preparation for the battle I was yet to face when Satan wanted to steal all those promises God had spoken over me.[31] However, this time, while I didn't always understand what I was going through at the time, I at least knew that God cared about me, was for me, and would be with me throughout the process.[32] It made all the difference in the world.

HIS STORY

The suspense rises
The plot does thicken
All the while, we're left chicken
The audience grows scared
They run in terror
Wondering if the script has an error
They run not far
But far enough to find
They're also in the film line
Why does life treat them so unkind?
They run to each other
In hopes that someone else knows what to do
Turning their backs on the Author Who could give them
a better view
Oh God, we're so blind
We can't see the big story

And repeat the same mistakes we see in books of history
Oh God, I pray
Help us to see the story through Your bigger view
Let us see the story isn't about us
It's about glorifying You

Reflect:

I CHALLENGE you to ask God to take you through the story of your life and change the narrative. God is the Author of your story. Ask Him His view of it and where He was in the midst of it. While you might have felt alone, we are never alone. He will never leave us nor forsake us.[33] The perspective in which you see your life and the narrative in which you speak over it[34] can make it or break it. Allow Him to be the cornerstone upon which every other thing in your life is built upon.[35]

What are the benefits of worshipping God? (Psalm 103 is a good place to start.) When I failed to see how much God loved me, though I never doubted His existence, my efforts to please Him were futile.

Hebrews 11:6 says: "But without faith it is impossible to please Him, for he who comes to God must believe that He is, and that He is a rewarder of those who diligently seek Him."

Contrary to what religion would say, we cannot please God while only believing in His existence. After all, even the demons believe and tremble.[36] We must move past the knowledge and fear of Him to believe in His benefits. I don't know of any person who would exercise and eat healthy without thinking there was something beneficial to it, yet religion would have us believe that it's selfish to worship God for anything other than who He is. While there's some truth to it, the real truth is that God's benefits and rewards are tied to Him. His rewards are a package deal. You cannot please Him without believing that He'll reward you for it.

Lastly, ask God to show you who He is. Ask Him to show you His goodness. Romans 2:4 says that it's God's goodness that leads us to repentance. While outward actions can change for a time through shame and fear, there will be no lasting change without a turning of our mind towards God's goodness. It is not God's will that any should perish.[37] He wants nothing more than to reveal who He is to us and through us. Here are just some of the names of who God is that can be found in Isaiah 9:6: Wonderful Counselor, Mighty God, Everlasting Father, Prince of Peace.

It doesn't stop there. Nothing good in this world[38] or in us[39] would exist apart from Him. Once we see clearly who our Creator is, the more we can see clearly who we are and everything else around us. The more we trust the Author of our story, the more we can see the direction in which to live our lives.

SECTION II

LOST

LOST IN THE WOODS

I'm lost in the woods
Could You bring me back
to You... would You?
I'm tired & I'm scared
And I feel all alone
And I'm trying to find You
I feel I've lost my way
I've come to a dead end
Wasn't I just here the
other day?
I'm going in circles again
'Cause I'm lost in the woods
And I know I need Your help
When I tried to find my way
on my own
I don't know what You
must've felt
But this day's turning into
night
And I don't want to be
stuck here forever
Help me find the way
Lead me to Your light
As this darkness closes in
I'm scared I'll spend
eternity without You
But then I hear Your sweet
whisper
Telling me to look within...
4 find You
I'm lost in the woods
But now I see a light
Please be my Guide
Lead me back to You

RACHEL JONES

3

DEFINE

"Define yourself radically as one beloved by God. This is the
true self. Every other identity is illusion. God's love for you and
His choice of you constitute your worth."
Brennan Manning

"What sorrow awaits those who argue with their Creator.
Does a clay pot argue with its maker?
Does the clay dispute with the one who shapes it, saying,
'Stop, you're doing it wrong!'
Does the pot exclaim, 'How clumsy can you be?'
How terrible it would be if a newborn baby said to its father,
'Why was I born?' or if it said to its mother,
'Why did you make me this way?'"
This is what the Lord says—
the Holy One of Israel and your Creator:
"Do you question what I do for my children?
Do you give Me orders about the work of My hands?

I am the one who made the earth
and created people to live on it."
Isaiah 45:9-12a (NLT)

"I have crossed the horizon to find you
I know your name
They have stolen the heart from inside you,
But this does not define you
This is not who you are
You know who you are"
Moana

I've watched *Moana* before, but this time was different. My eyes welled up with tears feeling as though God was whispering this is the way He speaks to us, the way He's spoken to me.

As mentioned before, when I tried to take my own life, I never stopped believing in God, but I had a hard time believing He wanted anything to do with me. I felt unloved and unwanted. I didn't know who to reach out to and bottled up everything inside. I didn't want to burden anybody.

The One who had always heard the cries of my heart and gave me purpose my entire life felt so distant and cold, and I questioned God's love for me. I questioned His goodness and didn't understand why He allowed me to go through the things I had.

I got pregnant with my first child two months after this and had an incredibly rough pregnancy—unable to hold down any food or water the first eighteen weeks. Despite that, the thought of life coming from me, someone who wouldn't have been here had my plans succeeded, felt like a gracious gift from God. It was probably the only thing that kept me from trying to take my life again at that point. While I loved my daughter immensely, life certainly didn't get easier upon her arrival or when I got pregnant again three months after she came. I tried so hard to be everything for my husband and new babies. I wanted to be the perfect wife and mom, yet I was drowning in sleepless nights of completely reversed schedules when I was sent to another room so we wouldn't disrupt the sleep of others. My body went into survival mode, and my body changed drastically under stress, sleepless nights, over-exercising, severely under-eating, undiscovered autoimmune deficiencies, and the shame I carried around from myself and others.

I wasn't wanted. I found out early on that infatuation and love are not one and the same, understanding that infatuation is unstable and unsafe. Fear and insecurity drove my actions. Failing to manipulate love, enduring so many hardships, and not wanting my kids to grow up seeing me so unlike myself, my courage grew enough to face the shame of divorce. There was no health, life, or love in our marriage. No hope either it would seem. Somehow the shame of attempted suicide seemed easier to handle despite people thinking I could go to hell if it was successful. My life already felt like a living hell, and I felt there was no hope of escape.

I was set to go to a women's retreat the day I felt certain I'd get divorced. It was the first time I got away by myself since being married. A sweet marriage counselor who had no idea of my situation told me she was praying and felt like God was going to use our story to help so many other marriages. I knew she was right. My husband and I had had so many prophecies and confirmations that we were supposed to be together at the beginning of our relationship for a reason. As she spoke to me, I broke down in tears while verbally vomiting all that was going on, probably making her wonder if she heard correctly. The words she shared with me that day caused me to hold on. Being able to open up to a sweet, gracious friend who was so empathetic to my newfound state helped me want to try again.

Unfortunately, but fortunately as well, my efforts didn't get me or us anywhere because I might have thought it was my doing if they had. God got ahold of us. I had to learn to set up healthy boundaries first, but God got ahold of my husband's heart when I was still choking on bitterness, hate, and unforgiveness towards him and others. I received so many God-breathed words from others that helped me survive during that time, but it wasn't until that time of fasting and prayer that God just utterly destroyed the box that I put Him in and overwhelmed me with His love. It was as though I was revisiting all these times in my life—the times I felt God so close and the times He felt so far away. God reminded me of the times He poured out His love towards me and showed me that He was always present, His heart towards me always good, and He was just waiting to lavish His love upon me. All those things God allowed me to go through were because He loved me just like He loved Jesus—like He loved Job and Joseph. Not once did He bring up the ugly, bitter woman I had become. Not once did God bring up my own sin or inconsistencies. Not once did He shame me. His goodness made my self-righteous attempts seem like the filthy rags[1] that Isaiah speaks about. His goodness led me to repentance.[2] He reminded me of who I am and who He created me to be. His thoughts towards me are far greater than anything I could imagine. They are truly for good and not for evil. He has plans to give me hope and a future.[3]

I was so used to hearing the voices of shame and condemnation spoken over me from myself and others. I had gotten comfortable with beating myself up and defining myself by my struggles. All the jabs I heard throughout my life that caused me to think there was something wrong with me deep down came flooding back into my memory. The more unloved I felt, the more those lies embedded into my spirit. Some of those lies were ones I never thought I had allowed to take root, but my present circumstances seemed to confirm them like a broken record played back repeatedly. Those lies I heard from others became my own thoughts, my own self-talk. The more rejected I felt, the higher the walls I built around myself. People I once had a heart for now seemed to be unsafe. The more I shut out love from entering my life, the more my own love grew cold and bitter. Forgiveness and hope seemed unreachable. Loving myself and trusting again felt impossible. Giving up seemed inevitable. As someone whose one pride was my tenacity and resilience, I hated myself for it. I had such a hard time forgiving myself for not knowing better, for not setting boundaries, for allowing my own nature to be affected so much by others' actions, and for making excuses in life. I was never one to look up to damsels in distress, and I didn't even know what role to play in my newfound story. I just found myself stuck and unable to move forward.

God never gave up on me. He showed me how He was there every step of my journey, standing in the fire with me. He loved me right then in my mess just as much as He loved me when I thought I was doing everything right and reminded me of the purpose He had planned for me. I had this overwhelming sense that I had to believe that I was His creation, and that He did a good job on me. I had to stop claiming that I was just a sinner or defining myself by my struggles because what I believed about myself to be true, my actions would live out of. If Satan can get us to question who we are, we won't know our mission or the role we were meant to play. It is so important we allow our Creator to show us our identity and purpose and believe Him at His Word. It is so important that we not only go back through our story from His perspective, but we allow Him to be our narrator in the process and follow the script He has for us.

WHEN I WAS FIRST BORN, I was celebrated as every life should be. While I think my parents were at the point that they wanted to be done having kids—after three hard losses and my mom bleeding in the third month of her pregnancy with me—my perfectly formed image on the first and last ultrasound she ever received probably brought her immense relief and hope. After three painful and discouraging hits to her heart, those feelings might have been even more heightened. The grateful tears she shed may have felt even more intense than the ultrasound I had with one of my daughters I bled with, fearing I lost her. Even better, my sisters firmly believed I was an answer to their prayers for a little sister, and they affirmed my worth as a young child. Growing up, I thought my parents' losses must have been brothers waiting for us in Heaven as my sisters adamantly prayed for a sister, and I was my parents' last child.

My girlhood was celebrated, and my foundations firmly set in the fact that God brought me into this world as an answer to prayer. My mom carried that perfectly formed ultrasound image that brought her so much joy with her in her purse everywhere she went. One day, her wallet was stolen from our big, red and white GMC van, the image with it. I heard about that loss for years and the joy she had in seeing my perfectly formed image for the first and only time since ultrasounds weren't as common back then. My identity was affirmed, and my life and femininity received as the gifts they are.

However, as I got older, womanhood seemed suffocating. The world, and especially religiosity, seemed to put such a box around women—one I never seemed to quite fit into. I was told I was too free-spirited, my body dangerous, and my voice too loud. I was too stubborn, not feminine, too feminist. I was too much of one thing while not enough of another. The list goes on and on. I think most women can relate to an extent. My dreams were never of getting rescued by a man. In most of the movies I grew up watching, I identified more with the strong male leads that gave up their lives to protect their countries or families. All my dreams centered around someone coming to rescue me, only for me to have already rescued myself or turning the heart of the man who captured me and partnering with him against a common enemy. As a child, it resulted in me trying to act like a tomboy and always trying to prove that I was just as capable as the boys around me. I took pride when I was told I threw like a boy, didn't drive like a woman, or was "one of the guys." I befriended both males and females who seemed to have an equal disdain for my own kind, yet I didn't like hearing guys put down their significant others either. I always tried to take the woman's side, whether I agreed with her actions or not.

When I heard and read about the glorified Proverbs 31 woman, I felt this great relief that I finally had a strong female to look up to. She seemed to do and have everything I wanted that God and others expected of women as well. I didn't look at her account as a threat or impossibility but as a challenge to live up to and conquer. I read every Christian book I could get my hands on to help me fulfill my newfound mission. After all, I was told my role as a woman was to be my husband's helpmeet and that women were created for men and to bear children. Whatever I did, I wanted to do it well and my best. I wanted my husband's heart to trust mine. I desired to do him good and not evil all the days of his life so he wouldn't have any lack of gain. Because of that, I saved my first kiss and so many other firsts for him. I worked out and strengthened my arms so that I was always fit to do whatever God asked of me. A guy that spoke at church said the greatest gift I could give my husband was to be without debt. When I met my husband, who was older and ready for marriage before I was done with college, I quit school to pay off my debt and save up for our wedding. When we got married, my entire life centered around him and meeting his needs in every possible way—making every meal, writing little notes I put in his lunch, keeping the house clean, the laundry done, always being physically available. It never seemed enough—for him or me. I lost my worth in everything I did.

The underlying messages I heard always seemed to portray that the message of grace was for men, not women. Men could live by grace, but women were judged by performance. I was commanded to respect men because of their gender, position, and need, yet I would only earn respect and love if I fulfilled a man's needs. Even then, I might be sarcastically put down and my worth as a female would always be defined by the careless men in my life. The people I looked up to and respected as leaders, I would hold to a higher standard. But males were given a pass to be leaders just for being males or ruthless with the idea that "boys will be boys." Normally, only bullies see the voices of the oppressed as a threat, but in some religious circles, it seemed to be acceptable to silence over half the population because it might make the men seem weak. If a woman did speak up, we might be seen as having a Jezebel spirit. When I got married, I did all the right things I was taught to do and then some, yet there was still no love. My husband was very much a taker and I a giver. When he did help, I would hear from him or others that he was so much better than the deadbeat men we knew and how lucky I was. I experienced early on that everything I did as a woman was expected, and anything my husband did was praised. As my weight fluctuated so much between pregnancies and health issues, my insecurities only grew as I endured countless insults and suggestions. As someone who already struggled with my self-worth, those messages only made the lies I heard that much louder and the strongholds I faced only that much stronger.

My desire to do good and right things came from a desire to please God, my husband, and family. However, over time, I also built my self-worth on those good and right things I did. When those good things failed me and were used against me, I believed my worth came crumbling down with them. My purity, actions, and reputation were all worthwhile efforts to build upon, but I should have never allowed myself to start building my identity upon them. I shouldn't have allowed the words of myself or others to ever grow louder than the words God had spoken over me. My identity has to rely on what my Creator says of me, my worth on the blood He shed for me. Anything and everything else are not stable or worthy to build upon. The more I know God, the more I know myself and my purpose. The more I live out who He created me to be and allow Him to cover over my shame, the more my identity is revealed.

I wanted so badly to please God with my life, to be worthy of His praise as it says in Proverbs 31:30: "Charm is deceitful and beauty is vain, but a woman who fears the Lord, she shall be praised." I realized the way I saw myself most of the time was built upon lies, though from an early age I had prayed that God would give me a spiritual makeover.

SPIRITUAL MAKEOVER

Looking in the mirror
Feeling a little inferior
She sits with tears in her eyes
'Cause she's never begun to realize
All her pain was formed from lies

Feeling she must look like Hollywood minority
Looking nice became top priority
But it's all done in vain
Oh, what some people do to cover up pain
And how much more visible the spiritual stain

> Oh, little girls
> Don't listen to this world
> As society screams lies
> I hope you realize
> True beauty…
> Is only found in Me
>
> So swallow your pride
> Lay it all aside
> I am blemish cure
> I will make you pure
> Let Me take over
> This is spiritual makeover
> True beauty
> For eternity

DESPITE THAT, it felt like my worth as a woman would always be something I would constantly be striving after. I tried to embrace the wisdom in the serenity prayer: "God, grant me the serenity to accept the things I cannot change, courage to change the things I can, and wisdom to know the difference." I couldn't change who God made me to be, but I could learn to accept it. In order to counteract the lies, I had to start speaking the truth over myself that I'll share with you.

You were created on purpose.[4] Your gender was no accident. Your timing was perfect. God doesn't make mistakes. You're here for a reason. Whether you were wanted or not by your parents, your Heavenly Father wanted you.[5] He knit you in your mother's womb.[6] He didn't pass you up or allow you to die.[7] You are fearfully and wonderfully made.[8] God is a God who desires to gather up the prodigal son[9] and His older brother as a hen gathers her children.[10] It hurts God's heart when His children do everything right out of an insecurity that they're unloved or act out of an insecurity that they're unloved. He just wants us to know we're loved unfathomably,[11] and that everything He has is offered to us.[12] He wants us to know that Jesus was just the first among many brothers and sisters[13] and wants us to walk out in the knowledge that we can do even greater things than He did through His Spirit.[14] That we can get free from the bondage of sin and death[15] as we walk in His Spirit and abide in Him.[16] All of creation is waiting for the revealing of the sons and daughters of God to take back what was once lost to us.[17] There's hope. Let His Spirit breathe life into you .[18]

If God can speak through an ass,[19] I think He can speak through me and even *Moana* too. Read those words knowing they were meant for you too. The testimony of Jesus is the spirit of prophecy.[20] What God has done for me and others, He wants to do for you. He prophesies through sons and daughters. He speaks through dreams and visions.[21] He sent spies just to save a prostitute and her family.[22] He was a friend to sinners—tax collectors and prostitutes alike, knowing full well He would be accused of being a glutton and drunkard[23] or of having a demon.[24] He disrupted social status and put the Gentiles and Jews, slaves and free, females and males all on the same page.[25] He had no intention of shaming the woman at the well with five husbands and living with a sixth[26] or the woman caught in adultery.[27] You are so much more than the fraction of a person people have seen of you or treated you. He is not afraid of your mess. He will not make fun of your attempt to clothe yourself [28] and has already provided a sacrifice.[29] He will not shame you coming out of the closet[30] or your struggle to love yourself by attempting to love someone like yourself. God wants to remind you who He created you to be—His original intentions for your life. If the thought of His love towards you doesn't move you to tears or give you undeniable joy and hope, there's so much more in store for you! As long as your heart's beating—no, as long as His heart's beating—there's hope. Please, don't ever give up. He's just waiting to overwhelm you with His love. Be open to receiving it. Once you know who He is, Whose you are and who you are, you can move on and find out what your mission is and the purpose for your life.

Reflect:

WHAT DOES God say about you? If you haven't heard a specific revelation, here are a few good places to start. Write them down. Claim them for yourself. Tape them or frame them in your bathroom and speak them over yourself as you look into the mirror. It's even more important that you dress yourself in the Word and put on the whole armor of God than for you to get physically ready for the day. However, both are beneficial. If you have faith in Christ Jesus and have accepted Him at His Word, these all pertain to you.

1. I am a child of God through my faith in Christ Jesus! (Gal 3:26)

2. God loves me just as much as He loves Jesus! (John 17:23)

3. I am an heir of God according to His promise! (Gal 3:29)

4. I am precious, honored, and loved by God! (Isa 43:3)

• • •

5. I am a sister to Christ! (Rom 8:29)

6. I am God's special possession and chosen by God to declare His praises! (1 Pet 2:9-10)

7. I am Christ's friend! (John 15:15)

You could go on and on, and you should. Look up "who I am in Christ verses" on Google or whatever search engine you use and prepare to be affirmed. Write down the verses and revelations that mean the most to you. Different verses will mean more to you in different seasons. All are important, and all are yours for the claiming.

MAKE ROOM

"When we judge others, we leave no room to love them."
Mother Teresa

Jesus answered, "The most important is, 'Hear, O Israel: The Lord our God, the Lord is one. And you shall love the Lord your God with all your heart and with all your soul and with all your mind and with all your strength.' The second is this: 'You shall love your neighbor as yourself.' There is no other commandment greater than these."
Mark 12:29-31 (ESV)

"I want you to learn to love yourself. You can't love others if you don't love yourself." I recognized the gentle whisper during my morning drive home from working out. It was spoken so sweetly, brought with so much clarity, yet the more I dwelt on it, the more terrified I became. I had always heard of "people loving themselves in the last days" spoken as a warning to the church. The thought of loving myself seemed to bring with it a sense of danger and even shame.

I had made up my mind that I wasn't deserving of love. I had made too many mistakes—things I felt I needed to bring back to God's attention. Mistakes He quickly seemed to remind me He had already forgiven and forgotten. However, I couldn't forget them. I had such a hard time forgiving myself. It felt impossible. I held myself to such a high standard. As I mentally went over my record of wrongs, I felt as if God were asking, "When am I going to be enough? When will you let My blood cover you? When will you place value on the one that I bought for such a high price?" That thought moved me to tears as God showed me that my inability to love myself wasn't from Him but an issue of pride and false humility on my part.

Knowing God from a young age, I had such high expectations for myself—ones that I set out to meet. They were done out of good intentions, yet as I mentioned before, they became the things I started building my identity upon. The more I grew in knowledge of God, the more I lived out what I thought He wanted from me, and the more puffed up I became in my mind. It was all so subtle, really. I would have said that I agreed that all have sinned and fallen short of the glory of God.[1] I had it memorized from an early age. However, deep down, I never believed that anything I did was ever that bad, and that belief allowed me to pass judgement on others. I was never one to pass much judgement on unbelievers as I didn't know how they would really know better. However, I passed judgement on fellow Christians I didn't think were as loving or as accepting as me and used 1 Corinthians 5:12 to justify myself. My false humility, my sense of what was right, and my actions blinded me to my own hypocrisy.

I started to confuse "righteousness" with right deeds instead of being in right standing with God. In my head, I believed that it's by "grace we have been saved through faith and that it's not of ourselves lest any man should boast."[2] However, in my heart, I had started thinking that maybe it was because I did those right things that I got approval from God. When I stopped believing that God loved me, those things that once seemed to come easy for me now seemed to be a struggle. I knew God to be real. I still feared Him and desired to follow Him, but it was out of an insecurity that I was unloved, rather than the security that I was loved. I felt like no matter what I did, it wouldn't be enough to please Him.

When Hebrews 6:4-6 came into my mind, I thought it must be speaking of me and condemned myself. I was enlightened, "saved," and filled with the Holy Spirit. I tasted the good Word of God, and I experienced God's miraculous power. Still, I was screwed up. My unmet expectations led to such a disappointment in myself that I didn't know how to move past it. I didn't realize just how far from grace I had strayed until I "messed" up and couldn't forgive myself. I didn't realize just how powerful I thought I was and sins were until I thought my mistakes were big enough to destroy God's plan for my life. I didn't believe that about others who did what would seem to be "bigger" sins, but I thought that about myself. I expected a level of perfection for myself that I never expected from others and a level of perfection that God never expected from me.

I didn't know how to love myself unconditionally. My ego was built on everything I did right, and I didn't know how to accept my fallen state. I didn't know how to accept from myself what God had already expected of me. Because I couldn't love and accept myself, imperfections and all, I couldn't accept it in others either. Because I couldn't love myself unconditionally, I couldn't love others unconditionally either.

When unjust things happened in my life, my pride masked itself as self-pity. I asked questions like "Why me?" rather than

"Why not me?" as though something I could have done would have prevented me from the wild but loving nature of God. When I was called to forgive those who didn't seek my forgiveness or who tried to force forgiveness from me in an unloving way, I felt I had a right to be angry, a right to demand, a right to be jealous, a right to be unforgiving and bitter. I started thinking that nobody deserved to be treated this way, and especially not someone who was making every effort to do everything right. My pride masked itself as self-righteousness.

When I couldn't forgive myself, it was because I had taken the place of judge in my life—a seat only God sits high enough to fill. When I hated myself, it was because I trusted my own lofty opinion more than God's opinion about me. When I accepted self-condemnation, it was because I trusted my knowledge of my situations more than God's. When I compared or judged others, I didn't measure them according to God's standard but according to mine. I didn't allow room to grow in my or others' lives because I was sitting too high upon the throne in my life. My view of God was limited to my own understanding. The God I had built up stretched no further than the corners of my own mind.

The thing about self-pity, self-righteousness, self-condemnation, self-consciousness, self-hatred, and even self-love is that they all have one thing in common—self. Worship of self is the "national religion of hell" as David Roper puts it. There's nothing wrong with loving myself. After all, God does too. To not care for or accept myself would be to not care for the work of His hands.

However, there is a problem when I can't see past myself to let God use me right where I am— no matter what physical, mental, or spiritual state I'm in. To argue with my Creator over His Word is pointless, yet I've found myself doing it more times than I can count. Insecurity isn't really humble at all. Besides taking care of my body, I have so little to do with it. I didn't create the shape of my nose, the color of my eyes, my voice, or the height of my body. To tear it down is to say God made a mistake. He knew how much it would stretch and change over the years, and what He says about it remains the same. Besides accepting His gift of salvation and letting His Spirit plant seeds inside my heart as I abide in Him, I have little to do with my salvation either. To argue that I'm not good enough doesn't argue with my doing but God's. I've gotten so hung up on myself, my mistakes, my body, my image because I didn't trust Him. I didn't accept His creation of me. I didn't accept that God was enough, that His death and resurrection finished the job He set out to do, which included my salvation. I might say that I believed in God, but really, I believed in my willpower to do what was right no matter the circumstance, or else I wouldn't have had such a hard time forgiving myself. I might say I was being humble, but I was the biggest person in my head and left little room for Him and others. Humility isn't at all about thinking less of ourselves, but rather it is thinking of ourselves less as C.S. Lewis shared.

When I asked God to do whatever it took to use my life to serve Him and others better, I thought He would want perfection from me. I thought it was the way I could be a role model for others. I built my life on everything I could do, yet God was looking for what He alone could do. If God's message had to do with what we could do, it wouldn't be good news at all. It would be like every other religion that says we can work our way to salvation. That's not the gospel message. He allowed me to go through a shaking to get me off the throne in my life—anything that I could argue was the cause of His love for me rather than His doing and His faithfulness.[3] I was so completely oblivious to how much I put a box around Him, myself, and others. I was completely unaware of the principalities of darkness at work in my life that caused me to sit in Heavenly places with no room for growth.[4] God showed me He needed to increase in my life, and I needed to decrease.[5]

REDUCE ME TO LOVE

I look at me
And hate what I see
A child of God
Smothered in hypocrisy
And how can I judge
When I don't judge myself?
And how can I point
My finger at someone else?
I take a look in
And see I'm to blame
I'm the only one
Deserving such shame
And I'm begging for forgiveness
I know I don't deserve
And I'm asking for a heart
I hope You can unearth
Because I know I need You
I know I need Your touch
I know what I'm asking
Might be too much
Because I need a new outlook
I need a new heart
I can't undo what I've done
But I'd like a fresh start
I want to be humbled
To think on things above
So Father, reduce me
Reduce me to love

THE LEAST I COULD DO

Eight steps to a better life,
How to be a great wife,
All these laws I've kept from my youth.
These aren't about me, I'm living for You!
Just do my best;
I'll be just fine.
I've got a ticket to Heaven,
Better get in line.
I'm gonna get dressed
In my Sunday best.
I'm gonna look good;
You'll be impressed.
I've done everything I can;
I'm Your best man.
Everybody knows
Where I stand.
I love those who love me.
Those who hate me are surely
Just filled with insecurity.
I work out,
I eat clean,
I do everything I can
To live green.
I do my part,
Yet I still look cool.
I follow all Your rules
And call it old-school.
Surely, You'll be impressed.
I've got a track sheet six feet long,
And nothing to confess.

Truly, I deserve this;
I kept Your list.
I even saved
My first kiss.
What?! Of course it's about You!
I did all the good *I* could do
Why are You saying
You're beginning to think
I'm looking more and more like
A pharisee?
Why are You calling me
To something *I* can't do,
Saying that's how I best glorify You?
I heard You're a God of love!
Nobody said tough love!
Not any club
I'm a part of.
Those sugar-coated messages
Were way easier to hear.
I felt so good
When they tickled my ears.
How dare You say
I can't do this on my own?
How is it good news
I can't do this alone?
You know me!
I don't like to depend on anybody!
How could You say I dried up and died
The second I disconnected from Your vine?
Everybody said I was living the life!
So, why aren't You satisfied?
How could You tell me
I was worshipping self-
The biggest idol of hell?

And why would You say,
The best *I* can do
Has never pointed to You?
That's all I ever wanted!
I wanted to follow Your call!
But what's in it for me,
If I gave up my all?
And took up my cross,
And followed You.
Let You be my boss;
The *least I* could do.
But that's what You want,
Isn't it?
To call all the shots-
Be the biggest hit.
Let me bask in Your glory,
As You walk before me.
And finally walk free,
From the chains that have bound me.
That's the reason You died.
May You be glorified.
If it's not about me,
Then You get the glory.

Reflect:

WHAT ARE some of the faces that pride has taken on in your life?

. . .

WHAT IS the definition of pride in the English dictionary? How about the Biblical definition?

WHAT ARE the differences and similarities?

SHOULD PRIDE EVER BE a reason to celebrate?

HOW DOES LOVING yourself as God loves you free you from pride?

HOW DOES ACCEPTING yourself allow you to move past yourself and onto others?

PRIDE IS something we all struggle with in one way or another. However, it's also one of the most difficult things to see. If you don't see an area of pride in your life, ask a close friend to lovingly share what you could be missing and be humble enough to receive it. If you do get difficult feedback, don't beat yourself up over it. Take it to God, cast your cares upon Him, and release them. Let God cover you with His blood and righteousness and accept His free gift of salvation.

5

STAY HUNGRY

"Stay hungry. Stay foolish."
Steve Jobs

"In order to eat, you have to be hungry. In order to learn, you have to be ignorant. Ignorance is a condition of learning."
Robert Anton Wilson

"Blessed *are* those who hunger and thirst for righteousness, For they shall be filled."
Matthew 5:6 (NKJV)

"She can have it instead of it being broken!" I insisted. With that suggestion, my parents gave whatever object my older sister and I were fighting over to me. I can't remember our ages or even what object we were fighting over now. However, I do remember we had just read about Solomon's wisdom over two women fighting over a baby after the baby of one of them died during the night. Solomon knew the baby belonged to the woman who wanted the baby alive even if it meant giving the child to someone other than herself.[1] Days later, as we were fighting, I had the notion my parents were trying to teach us a lesson and see who was actually listening enough to apply our knowledge. I met the challenge.

MY DAD WORKED nights when we were young, so if we wanted to stay up, we could play with my mom's hair while she read the Bible to us. While I found it somewhat annoying, the Christian radio station and sermons were on at all times. Even if I tried to ignore it, those words spoken were constantly ingrained into my head. By first grade, I was in a Baptist school with the rest of my siblings. By the middle of the eighth grade, I transitioned to a Christian school when my previous school was shut down. I honestly don't remember missing a Sunday at church growing up. When I was younger and had to sit with my parents and dress up despite all the other kids being able to dress any way they wanted, I found it frustrating. However, as I got older and made friends, I had a little more freedom with my dress code and got filled with the Holy Spirit. By then, I went to church or youth group or whatever event the church had going on whenever I got the chance—sometimes going as often as two or three times a week. I constantly filled my mind with Scripture and Christian books about other people's understanding of

Scripture and what it means to be a Christian. I completely bought into the purity movement and encouraged others to do the same. Being the youngest of five and having the privilege of learning from my siblings' mistakes and always striving for excellence, I was constantly told I was wise beyond my years. I can't say that it didn't have an effect on me. While I would have never admitted to it or even believed it at the time, I think deep down I thought I had all the answers—maybe not all the experiences but at least the knowledge to know what was right. Even worse, I thought I was supposed to know it all.

Scripture was often used as a means for debate. My love for discussion and knowledge grew into a love of being right. "Getting people saved" was spoken of as Christian duty. A formulaic collection of verses was given in an effort to lead people to salvation. I was taught the "right" way to live, while those outside of my circles struggling in sin were clearly following the "wrong" path. If those "sinners" rejected our plan of salvation (our version of our path to God), they were often deemed evil or unknowing. Thank God for us know-it-alls (insert hand-to-forehead emoji here). It was us and them, not "we" humans. Growing up in a strict, oftentimes cold religious environment allowed me to have a deeper understanding of those who rejected our message. Sometimes I even admired those who lived so courageously and freely as their own person. I think it was due to the fact that my own ego, perfectionism, and desire to be right wouldn't allow me the freedom to act "wrongly" without shame and condemnation. My identity was so wrapped up in God and my ability to know and do what was "right." I couldn't even comprehend how people found an identity apart from that. I never experienced an environment free from shame or criticism as those who knowingly rejected God. At the same time, I also felt entirely sad and compassionate towards "outsiders," knowing where that rejection led to. My admiration and love for people entirely different from me often led to me being told I was "too free spirited" for not condemning others and their behavior or even a fellow Christian whose standards weren't up to our own. I took it as me being more loving and Christ-like, and in turn, I judged those Christians who should "know better" as I thought I did. In fact, as shared previously, I thought the Bible encouraged it.

As God started breaking down the religious walls I had built up, He showed me just how little righteousness has to do with being right and how it had absolutely everything to do with being right with Him.

THE RIGHT ONE

We sit in lines
With empty eyes
And a program that can't soothe
Our hearts' cries
And we wonder what You meant
When You became flesh
And dwelt among men
Never lacking in grace
Never lacking in truth
Yet, we think we show You
By all the "rights" that we do
We're feeding off yesterday's bread
Eating crumbs of yesteryear's meat
Unaware You offer fresh manna daily
As we sit at Your feet
And we read You meet needs
You set captives free
But we're busy hiding the chains
We don't want seen
So we hide behind a smile

Yet we're naked in Your sight
We ignore any thoughts
Of this being a spiritual fight
We're blinded by principalities of "rightness"
So desperate, we welcome Satan's kiss
No great relationship is about doing everything right
But rather, abiding with the One who is

My sense of my own rightness began to bury my lack of understanding. It created a boredom in what more could be learned and a satisfaction where there should be none. It makes one feel full when one should always remain hungry. I think the biggest sign of religious pride in my life came when I started thinking I had more answers than questions, when I thought my finite mind was capable of holding the infinite knowledge of God and the universe. To continually seek God and grow, one must always remain hungry—hungry to keep seeking, growing, and asking questions. It is only when we keep questioning the One that holds the answers with the assumption that we know nothing that we can arrive at the truth.

QUESTIONS OF EXISTENCE

Everyone's bound to have an off day,
But what about more than two?
What if you spent the last few years
Realizing off-days are what got you through?

What do you consider an accomplishment?
How do you measure success?
What questions of life are you answering
When ignoring the Creator's test?

Why do you drown out the silence
Whenever your thoughts run too deep?
Why do you ignore Purpose' whisper
When asking you to take faith's leap?

Why does loneliness hurt you so?
Seeking happiness from meaningless lovers
And when you find they're just as selfish
You go searching for another?

And how do you view yourself?
Is happiness only found with perfect body size?
Then why are countless models killing themselves
After listening to society's lies?

Have you ever wondered what you're seeking
When your soul always hungers for more?
What are your reasons for living
When you have nothing you would die for?

Is life supposed to be an endless chase
To reach happiness on the "come-and-go?"
And while going this false route
Why does your conscience hurt you so?

Is life meant to be this painful?
Is love supposed to hurt?
After living your meaningless life
Do you just decay into dirt?

When you don't know where you're heading
Which direction should you go?
Are these questions you'd like to keep asking
Or would you really like to know?

And if someone found true answers
Would you take it as reason enough?
And would you be willing to keep on going
When the going gets real tough?

And what if one that found Truth
Said Jesus is the only way
Would you follow 'til it wasn't so easy
And then again be led astray?

And now that you've heard truth
Have you counted the cost?
Between a life of gain
And a life always lost?

What's it going to be,
Your response to His call?
Will you live a life worth living?
Or one worth nothing at all?

Reflect:

When we feel full, we don't seek. Hunger points to a need. We all have needs that have to be filled that only God can fill.

What are some questions you have for God?

. . .

In what areas do you feel like you can grow? How are you going about it?

Do you feel "hungry" for God and His Word? If you answered no, why do you think that is?

At the beginning of each day, I encourage you to ask God to show up. Ask Him where He is, what He's doing, and how you can be involved. Ask Him what He wants to share with you about who He is. We all have so much more we can learn about our wondrous God and His infinite wisdom He wants to impart to us.

In the next chapter, I'm excited to share with you how our hunger can lead to us being filled.

SECTION III

BROKENNESS

I knew a girl once
who did the greatest impression
of a mannequin.
Her plastered smile
was always appealing,
and her painted mask
always just right.

Well, I saw her recently,
and her plastered smile
was revealing
the chipped glue underneath.
Her smile was no longer
plastered anymore.
Her face paint was smearing
with tears she'd never met before.
As a mannequin,
she had never been so broken;
but she never felt
so *real* in her life.

"Mannequin" by

6

FILL UP

"For He satisfies the longing soul,
and the hungry soul He fills with good things."
Psalm 107:9 (ESV)

"Addiction begins with the hope that something 'out there' can
instantly fill up the emptiness inside."
Jean Kilbourne

"If we do not fill our mind with prayer, it will fill itself with
anxieties, worries, temptations, resentments,
and unwelcome memories."
Scott Hahn

It was the summer of 2008. I was seven months pregnant with my first child when my husband and I had decided to move closer to family. My husband got a job at a charter school in inner-city Indianapolis and was starting in two weeks, and the little town we were living in got hit extremely hard with the market crash. Our options were staying with my parents while trying to sell our home three hours away or my husband making a six hour commute each day. We opted to stay with my parents in the tiny room I grew up in—with an entire furniture set that included a small double bed and mattress that was many decades old. There wasn't a lot of walking room with the crib next to our bed within arm's reach, and we weren't the only ones living there with my parents at the time. While we were so grateful to be without a second mortgage and for my parents letting us stay the entire year it took us to sell our house without rent, to say it was a challenge would be an understatement. One night, I got so frustrated that I started a journal to my daughter and told her all the things I hoped to do differently than my parents. Of course, what one dwells on, one ends up doing. It didn't turn out well.

Possibly that same night, I had a very vivid dream that sent chills up my spine for months. It was the middle of the night, and the house was swept and put in order. I went to my parents' backdoor to close the garage, only for a demonic presence to be staring at me behind the glass. As I reached for the door handle, so did he. I froze in panic. As I did, I saw him motioning for seven other more terrifying beings in the alleyway. I awoke in fright. The more I prayed about it after the fact, the more I felt like it was a warning. I was reminded of the parable Jesus told in Matthew 12:43-45:

> When an unclean spirit goes out of a man, he goes through dry places, seeking rest, and finds none. Then he says, 'I will

return to my house from which I came.' And when he comes, he finds *it* empty, swept, and put in order. Then he goes and takes with him seven other spirits more wicked than himself, and they enter and dwell there; and the last *state* of that man is worse than the first. So shall it also be with this wicked generation.

I had the strongest sense that filling up the empty, clean space with grace was needed if I didn't want something more sinister to fill it. That truth will never leave me.

There are so many religions that speak of emptying oneself and one's mind. It seems so wise. Yet the more I dwelt on emptying myself of everything negative in my life, the more I saw those things come out of me. It left room for other toxic things to fill that space.

Around that same time, I watched a video someone shared of a water bottle with dirt settled on the bottom. As a faucet was turned on and clean water began filling the bottle up, the entire thing became filled with mucky water as the dirt rose to the top and scattered around. It almost looked as if the clean water was actually making it dirtier. Over time though, as the water continuously poured in and the mucky water continued to rise and spill out, the water got clearer and clearer. Eventually, the entire bottle was filled with clear water. It took some time, but as I watched it happen, I felt as though God gently whispered to my spirit, "I will never leave you empty."

The more I thought about it, the more I realized just how true that statement was. While other religions speak of emptying oneself, God speaks of filling us up with good things. He so often reminds us in Scripture that He left His Holy Spirit to live within us. While so often we're taught to dwell on the negative, God tells us to meditate on whatever is good, noble, just, pure, lovely, of good report, virtuous, and praiseworthy.[1] He told us to fix our eyes upon Jesus and eternal things.[2] God knew that whatever we dwell on and fill ourselves up with will eventually pour out from us.

God never speaks of us emptying ourselves but rather filling ourselves with good things. God's way of meditating has to do with mindfulness, not mindlessness. As His pure living water fills our lives, those ugly sins and messes we've gotten ourselves into often rise to the top and scatter around, making it feel so impossible to see clearly just like in the bottle illustration. So often during that time, we just want to give up. We think maybe it was better before we heard God's truth, maybe it's easier to stay trapped in sin. Every time we try to quit lying or lusting or drinking, we end up disappointed and ashamed of ourselves. We grow comfortable with the mess in our lives, and we settle because it seems easier than doing the hard work of allowing God to continually pour into our lives, exposing the messes we got ourselves in. It feels so much easier to stay bound than to fight for our freedom.

BOUND

What did I get myself into?
These steel chains are too difficult to undo
How did I ever stray from Your plan?
I'm hating everything I am
My God, my God, please forgive me
Show me Your unfailing mercy
Get me out of this mess
I'm afraid I'm settling for less
How do I break these chains I've made
When I've wandered off the path You've laid?
My weakness has become my biggest sin
And I'm binding myself again
Many friendly souls warned me of this road I'm on

FILL UP

> I'm afraid to turn back; I'm too far-gone
> The strength I need is the strength I lack
> And I don't have enough for the journey back
> Free me from these chains that bind me
> Take away the will inside me
> Lead me back from where I left
> I don't want to settle for less
> I'm too far away from home
> Bound with chains I created on my own
> What did I get myself in?
> I'm binding myself again

RATHER THAN SETTLING with one's mess, rather than dwelling on all the toxic, negative things we all have that are too overwhelming to conquer solely on our own, God wants to replace them one truth delivered in love at a time. He doesn't subtract or take away from our lives. He always adds, multiplies, and substitutes with truth so we can live an abundant life. God has only—and always—wanted the best for us, and we can trust Him. His truths might seem hard to swallow or adapt our lives around. Our weaknesses and sins might rise to the top as He fills us with His living water, but they lead to our clarity and freedom. It will all be worth it in the end. May we allow God to pour into our lives, renew our minds, and substitute His truths for the toxicity that has clouded our perspectives and bound us to those very things that destroy us.

SUBSTITUTING THE ABSOLUTES

> How easily we substitute
> Every lie for every absolute

Because we're free to believe
Our own truth
How easily we've been deceived
Every religion clashing with what we believe
Forming different beliefs by every book we read
Every example we see
And every person proclaiming truth
With opinion
We think to be free
Means to state our mind
Claim our rights
And we ignore the liberty
That Jesus Christ died to set us free
And we're binding our own wrists
We're banging our fists
We're chaining ourselves down
But all the while, we're claiming
A new freedom we've found
Because love,
Yeah love makes the world go 'round
Or at least that's how musicians put it
And we believe every minute of it
And there's maybe some truth to it
But the truth is, we've substituted
Fact with feeling
Separation from God with healing
And it's got me wondering
When did the serpent speak to us?
Or did he ever leave us?
Because we're substituting
People with God
Beauty with immodesty
Worshipping with TV
And I don't think we even realize

We're being deceived
Lust of the flesh
Lust of the eyes
The pride of life
Satan always appears as an angel of light
And somehow, we think
He has our best intentions in mind
Because nobody, not even the devil
Could be so evil
Murderer, Thief, Father of Lies
Stealer, Killer, Destroyer
He's got us all blind
And somehow we've substituted
Satan's lies
For Jesus Christ
Now's the time to open our eyes
Substitute the absolute lies
With absolute Truth

Reflect:

WHAT ARE some areas of your life you feel like God is holding out on you? It could be singleness, marriage, infertility, a job, etc.

WHATEVER AREA that you thought of, I want you to go to Google and type in "Bible verses on (insert area here)" or "(area) Bible verses." Pray that God speaks to you through whatever you read.

Next, read the first page of verses listed on that subject. Some sites might have five while others might have 50+. I'd encourage you to at least read the one with the most as you never know which one might speak to you.

Now, whatever verse(s) stood out to you the most, write them down on a notecard or piece of paper. Tape it to your bathroom mirror, coffeemaker, or someplace you will at least see first thing in the morning and right before you go to bed.

Dwell on that verse(s). Don't just read it to get it over with each morning. Think through what it's saying, dwell on its meaning, say it out loud until you believe it in your heart and can say it from memory.

As doubts creep in and uncertainty grows about God and His plans for your life, remind yourself of Jeremiah 29:11: "For I know the plans I have for you," declares the LORD, "plans to prosper you and not to harm you, plans to give you hope and a future.

Also, remember Numbers 23:19: "God is not human, that He should lie, not a human being, that He should change His mind. Does He speak and then not act? Does He promise and not fulfill?"

Now, remind yourself of the verse(s) you wrote down regarding your specific circumstances. If that doubt and uncertainty coming into your mind doesn't line up with those verses, it is not coming from God and cannot be trusted. It's coming from the father of lies who comes to kill, steal, and destroy your life. One cannot listen to and serve both. It's up to you who you choose to listen to and follow.

7

CHOOSE

"And if it seems evil to you to serve the Lord, choose for yourselves this day whom you will serve, whether the gods which your fathers served that *were* on the other side of the River, or the gods of the Amorites, in whose land you dwell. But as for me and my house, we will serve the Lord."
Joshua 24:15 (NKJV)

"No one can serve two masters. Either you will hate the one and love the other, or you will be devoted to the one and despise the other. You cannot serve both God and money."
Matthew 6:24 (NIV)

"Do not worship any other god, for the LORD, whose name is Jealous, is a jealous God."
Exodus 34:24 (NIV)

"If you don't forgive me, then God won't forgive you." The harsh, yet truthful threat stabbed my heart over and over again each time it was said. I wondered how a loving God could not only bring the insensitive perpetrator into my life but make it painstakingly obvious He led us on our journey together after some other very trying circumstances He led me through.

For most of my life, I had felt God had chosen me from birth. That knowledge was my one comfort when I felt unknown, unloved, or rejected. God knew me, loved me, and accepted me —that was enough. I trusted that whatever course I took in life, He was with me and would use it for my good because I loved Him and was called according to His purpose.[1] Loving and choosing the one steady Constant in my life who wanted what was best for me was easy. In fact, it felt like I had no real choice but to love Him back. In a way, that was part of the problem.

You see, it isn't difficult to choose to be in a relationship with someone when it's easy. However, love has nothing to do with ease, and love doesn't stem from force. It has to come from a place of freedom or free will as we know it. Love has to come from choice. God knows this. Even the makers of *Aladdin* know this.

Anyone can imitate love for a while. Narcissists can even give the impression that they care for a time. However, the feelings will not last if one feels forced or deceived into loving another. No depth will grow out of the shallow sand of ease. No relationship will stand the test of time if grown out of the hardened soil of indoctrination. No love will blossom that stems merely from the surface. Love has to come from a choice to remain even when it's hard. Choosing to keep our gaze steadfast is necessary when presented with trying times.

Love doesn't come naturally for us. It has to be decided upon each and every day. God wants to be chosen every single second. He wants to be trusted, known, loved, and accepted even when we're led down a difficult path. God is an all-consuming fire, and a jealous God[2] who wants to be wanted and chosen just like we do. The decision then becomes this: Will we trust in who God says He is and what His intentions are for us when the enemy tries to deceitfully change the narrative about Him and us during the process?

FOR THE FIRST time in my life, I wasn't so sure I wanted to choose God. I didn't feel secure in His love for me. I didn't think He could possibly have my best in mind anymore, and I was angry. He led me down such a painful path, and the thought that He wouldn't forgive me if I didn't forgive those who intentionally seemed to hurt me infuriated me. It seemed so unjust. God's existence was without question, but it was no longer comforting. It became a maddening irritation and annoyance I couldn't rid myself of. As I unwittingly blocked out God's love, a poisonous root of bitterness dug its relentless claws around the chambers of my heart and a constant battle was fought for my mind.

Truth, love, and God's goodness no longer filled my being. I made way and left room to be tormented by spirits of fear, unforgiveness, and self-pity. As I held onto my right to be angry and hurt, I became attuned to choosing self-protection and anger over my desire to surrender to a God I no longer trusted had my best in mind. It felt like I was finally growing up in a way—no longer naive to the indoctrination of my youth.

I wanted so desperately to go back to my naivety and childlike innocence, to believe everything I did at the beginning, but my heart was so far from God. Over and over, I chose to listen to the lies that He couldn't be trusted, and that I had to take matters into my own hands and build up a wall of self-protection because no one else cared about me. I betrayed God and our relationship when He sought my trust the most.

BETRAYAL

Never-ending Love,
I turned my back on You.
I took back a promise that I swore I'd never do.
So selfish am I;
So faithful are You.
You wipe back tears from gentle eyes
And hide the pain I put You through.
You, who are so caring and trustworthy,
How could such omniscient Love put such faith in faithless me?
My Love...can I call you that...my Love?
When all my actions, my priorities,
show You are not the One I think of?
You still won't give up on me, will You?
You would still die for me when You knew I would deceive You.
You knew I would be one to nail You to that tree
over and over again.
You knew I would not give up on my selfish lust of sin.
Here I am in that old place again,
Down on my face again.
These words are not new.
These sins I wish I over-grew.
Here am I, so childlike; or rather, childish.
My lack of innocence betrays me, but oh how I wish.
I wish for my life to be anew.
I wish for the days of faithfulness to You.
Oh God, make me more like You.
I'm tired of all I put You through.
I would ask You for a less difficult task

Because I know I'm not one to accomplish what You ask,
But I know that would never do with You.
You have given me an even greater one,
Not because You know I owe You,
But because You trust me to have Your will be done.
And I have never been so grateful to be indebted to You.
My Love, I cannot accomplish this without You,
And I will not even begin to try
Like I should have done from the first time.

WHILE I WRESTLED with thoughts and accusations about God that clearly didn't come from Him, He patiently waited for me to choose Him again. He didn't force Himself upon me. He didn't argue with my thoughts or butt-in with rude demands. God didn't raise His voice and shout against the loud accusations swirling in my mind saying that He wasn't all I had cracked Him up to be in the past. In fact, it often felt as though God wasn't present at all. I knew that couldn't possibly be true, but it was as though He respectfully hid Himself while He waited to see if He was wanted. Like a true gentleman, He pursued me, but then held Himself back as He let me figure out my level of involvement or whether I wanted to be involved in a relationship at all. All the while, I tried so desperately to remind myself of the things I knew to be true when I was a child. I sought to tune out the lies and go back to the foundations my entire life was built upon and to the love of my youth. When God knew He was wanted, He showed up ready to lavish His love upon me again and reminded me why I fell in love with Him in the first place.

Reflect:

THIS MIGHT REQUIRE a bit of time for some of you, but I want you to take the time to just stop and think. What is it that brought you to God in the first place?

DO you feel like you actually chose God at some point in your life, or do you feel like you just grew up believing in Him from your childhood, never actually having made the personal choice to follow Him?

IF YOU FEEL like that's the case and you've often wondered why He seems so distant, I'd encourage you to take the time now to let God know that you choose Him. Pray it in silence, out loud, or write it down. Do whatever you need to do or what feels most meaningful to you. God knows the desires of your heart and just wants you to acknowledge and choose Him.

In this chapter, we learned that God is a jealous God who wants to be wanted. He's not going to compete for our time, money, or attention if we don't want Him around. Sometimes God does sit back in silence as we're being tested. However, sometimes God is just waiting for us to decide if we really want Him involved. Other times, God might need to remind us how much He has always loved us so we can choose to return to Him.

8

RETURN

"I know your works, your toil and your patient endurance, and how you cannot bear with those who are evil, but have tested those who call themselves apostles and are not, and found them to be false. I know you are enduring patiently and bearing up for My name's sake, and you have not grown weary. But I have this against you, that you have abandoned
the love you had at first."
Revelation 2:2-4 (ESV)

"Maybe your first love is the one that sticks with you because it's the only person who will ever receive all of you. After that, you learn better. But, most of all, no matter what, a piece of you forever remains left behind in the heart of the one you loved- a piece no future lover could ever get, no matter what. That piece holds innocence, the belief that love really can last forever. It holds friendship and pain, trial and error, that one kiss you'll never forget, and that night under the stars you can never get

back. It holds youth and everything you thought love would be, everything that was proven wrong."
Arif Zubair

"All at once everything looks different, now that I see you."
Tangled

---

*T*ears streamed down my face the other week on the twelve-hour drive back to my hometown in Indianapolis. My kids were watching a movie in the back while I was watching the beautiful plains, tall grasses, and rolling hills. In an instant, a flashback I had long forgotten hit me of a time when I was in middle school on my way to Illinois with a close friend who was like family to me. I had just ended my first real relationship. Although, in reality, it was more of a pen-pal-ship.

Though I had met "Phil" at a church camp in inner city Philly, his parents were missionaries to England at the time where he was also living. The first year we met, he and his friends hung out with me and mine. Phil was cute and shy with the sweetest puppy dog eyes. I think he actually thought my friend was cute, who was slightly more his age, but after we talked for a bit, he seemed to be interested in me. I was the youngest attendee in the camp at twelve and a half—which was more like twelve and a third, but I had to beef it up a tad since you're supposed to be at least thirteen to attend. Phil was two years older than me.

At the time, I was just a chubby girl with braces who hoped that any guy I liked would think I had the possibility of growing into looking like one of my gorgeous sisters that every guy seemed to like. I didn't want a lot of interest or even care for a guy who was popular with other girls. One guy's interest was more than enough for me. The fact that Phil even thought I was cute amidst my beautiful friends made me feel special. The more we wrote—yes, actual letters back then—the more our interest seemed to grow. At one point, Phil sent me a phone card so we could talk since it was long distance with him living in another country. The 15-digit number is still etched in my memory even after all this time.

In his letters, Phil often sent me pictures to share his life with me. They were pictures of him, but also pictures of beautiful flowers at their ministry in England. Phil would write that since he couldn't send me real flowers, a picture of them would have to do. He told me how his trip to Switzerland with his dad made him think it was the most beautiful country he had been in at the time. I would look up pictures on our slow, dial-up internet and picture myself there with Phil, happily frolicking on the mountainside. I'm not going to lie, I still hope to visit one day, but he's not in the picture anymore. His life just seemed so exciting, unlike my own. I didn't understand why he was even interested in me.

One day, Phil asked what my favorite kind of chocolate was, and I had absolutely no idea. I had never really eaten any chocolates besides candy bars, so I asked my older brother how I should respond. My brother told me to say Godiva chocolate. The name sounded elegant and like something other girls might like but not at all who I was. Phil didn't know how to get that, so instead, he sent me a package with pretty much every kind of candy he could possibly get from England or other places he traveled. There were all types of candy bars—many I had never heard of. I thought it was so sweet that I don't think I ever ate a single one for fear of throwing them away.

I was absolutely sure I was going to marry the kid, making my initials R.A.P. I liked rap music at the time, though I dared not tell my parents. Our favorite chips were both sour cream and onion. His favorite ice cream was chocolate chip cookie dough, which was my second favorite. He was into drawing like me. I even childishly drew a portrait I sent him from the picture I had taken of him and his friends. Thankfully, Phil never made fun of me for that. My innocent little mind had decided our meeting was fate and that we were destined to be. I felt lucky I had met "the one" at such a young age.

I think at the time, I just felt safer with Phil emotionally than I felt with any other guy I had ever met. He seemed to care about me as much as I did him. The fact that he liked me and seemed to notice me at a time I didn't feel in the least bit attractive made such an impression upon my little heart. The one crush I had ever admitted to years before I ever met Phil—as I was always too scared to really share any crushes for fear of rejection—was teased and made known by my older brother. Later, I overheard my crush's older sister saying how if I didn't annoyingly laugh so much, I might be ok or something along those lines. This relationship with Phil was far from that feeling.

However, as time went by without seeing each other, it seemed Phil's interest began to fade. I remember the day I had to get four of my teeth taken out and was told he was going to call me. It was such a big deal in those days, and it had been so long since we'd talked, so I was ecstatic. But then I realized how numb my mouth was. I knew when Phil called, I'd be a drooling, mumbling ugly mess. The thought brought me to tears. Sadly, he never did call that day. Part of me was thrilled because of my circumstances, the other part was hurt. It seemed Phil was losing interest while others' interest in me was growing. I always held out hope that maybe he was just busy with ministry and didn't have time for me only to later wonder if I should keep my options open for fear of disappointment.

Over time, a mutual friend of ours was visiting from Pennsylvania and actually called me during his visit to England. "Al" was concerned for Phil. He shared how Phil's dad was always busy with ministry and left Phil with little attention. He had gotten involved with the wrong crowd and started smoking. The fact that Al called me was a big deal because it showed Phil still talked about me. While I wasn't thrilled about the crowd he was hanging around or some of the unhealthy habits he had picked up, I tried to overlook those facts.

I learned Phil was going to finally go to the same camp we where we met two years before, and it was like we almost picked up where we left off. Except now, he had picked up smoking and I had thinned out and gotten my braces off. I was excited to see Phil again, especially now that I looked different, and he had liked me at my worst. He told me absence makes the heart grow fonder, and I completely agreed and tried to forget the long pause we had or that I cared about health and smiles and wanting to live a long, healthy life together. I already felt myself starting to compromise for him. In my gut, I knew it was a sign, but I completely ignored it. However, a close friend of mine I really admired that drew me closer to God spoke up about it. She felt like God was wanting me to give Phil up as a sacrifice like Abraham had to Isaac. She was sure God would provide the sacrifice if it was meant to be. With how deeply I cared about him, it felt a lot like a sacrifice. But more than anything, I wanted what God wanted and felt at peace about ending it. That is, until I saw him again.

Phil's friends made it very apparent they knew all about me. His younger brother said something to the fact that Phil had told him he couldn't believe how pretty I was upon seeing me again. I didn't realize just how hard it was going to be. I had set out to focus on God during this camp like I had the year Phil wasn't there, only to be completely consumed by thoughts of him. It terrified me. I wasn't sure how I was going to end it or if I could. I had to make a concerted effort to focus on God, our outreaches, the community we were serving, and my friends. I always kept coming back to Phil despite him hanging out with people I wouldn't usually hang out with as much and probably looking like one of the "bad guys" to my church group with his big baggy jeans, backwards cap, and marker-drawn tattoos. He didn't smoke in my presence, but one of my friends got away a few times to go smoke with him and his friends. It made me a little uncomfortable to see her so flirtatious with him, but Phil didn't seem to bat an eye towards her.

When we were doing a prayer walk around the neighborhood, he came up beside me and asked if he could hold my hand, mentioning how his grandparents started off slower like that. It melted my heart and made me feel so valued that he'd even ask. My heart skipped a beat since I had never held hands with a boy before. Even still, I told him I didn't think it was appropriate then because I truly didn't. This wasn't what I was prepared for or how I thought it'd be. It was supposed to be easier than this. All those thoughts of it not being able to work out went out the window when he bought me a camera.

It sounds silly, but Phil spoke my love language—in the form of gifts—better than anyone I ever met. That stinking camera threw all my caution and preparation to end whatever it is we had out the window.

I always took a ton of pictures during camp and brought four rolls of film, only to find out my camera didn't work on the very first day. I was devastated. When Phil learned of it, he got one of the kids from the rough neighborhood our camp was stationed in to take him to a nearby store and bought me not one but two disposable cameras. He wrapped them in the plastic bag and handed them to me when we were at an outreach. When I opened the bag, it took me by such surprise that I thanked him and squeezed him. Our first actual touch was a hug after two years of whatever we had, and it felt so good. It was completely unplanned by me and was reprimanded by one of our new youth group leaders until another leader explained the situation. While she apologized, I still felt awful and ashamed because I had made up my mind that I was going to end whatever Phil and I had before it began again. I wanted to put God first, and I felt like He was asking me to. I did a fun and silly dance with a friend of mine and saw Phil looking at me in what seemed to be awe and after he shared what a great dancer he thought I was. I had never had that before. I never felt so loved or accepted. I reasoned with God that breaking up with Phil wasn't a good idea only to have such a strong feeling that I needed to. I had stayed up trying to write my reasonings for ending whatever we had and handed it to him, only to learn from a friend of his that he was planning on officially asking me to be his girlfriend that very day and sobbed. He came over and just hugged and held me. After I had just told him and explained why we couldn't be together, Phil was concerned about me and my feelings. I never felt so safe and yet so torn as I did right then in his arms. I no longer cared what anyone thought about it.

I didn't know if I cared if it was meant to be or not. I wanted so badly to make it happen. I told myself that I liked the smell of smoke. I justified that he'd just gotten into things I didn't approve of as a result of not getting attention. We didn't need to have the same goals in life or hang around the same crowds. His parents were missionaries, so of course he cared about God. And even if he didn't, he cared about me, and I assumed he'd care more about God eventually. He cared about *me*. Someone I liked, someone I deeply cared about, seemed to have mutual feelings for *me*. It was such a crazy concept for me to believe. I never felt worthy.

When I was on that trip with my lifelong friend to Illinois for her family reunion the same summer I saw Phil again, I saw those tall grasses and rolling hills and started picturing my young love and I running through them just as I had when he first told me of Switzerland. I saw this picture of my future self as being delighted in and free. I realized then it could never happen with him, that our future couldn't be a healthy one, and that my effort and his great ability to speak my love language didn't have the power to make it work, especially without God. My young love was my Isaac all right, and I had to truly let go of my desire to hold on to someone so tightly that wasn't meant for me. It was the first and only relationship that I actually had to burn so many memories of in order to move on, and my fourteen-year-old mind decided then and there that I never wanted to feel so deeply for another until I knew for sure that I was going to marry him.

Within a year, I started another two-year long-distance relationship (probably my way of protecting myself and an excuse to not let the guys in who kept trying to pursue me within a closer proximity). This time "Lee" was the one who set the higher standard. We read "Passion and Purity" by Elizabeth Elliott together per his suggestion, and he wanted to take things slowly and seek God through it all. Lee was pretty much every dad's dream because our relationship left little room for worry. At the time, I was only fifteen and he was eighteen. His family's standard was that he wasn't allowed to date until adulthood, so I was his first relationship. I had "potential for marriage," and maybe Lee wanted to lay stakes on me so to speak, but he also wanted me to be able to have the same chance to find myself as he'd had since he couldn't date until he was older. Plus, if it wasn't meant to be, we could look our spouses in the eyes and not feel regret when we looked back and shared about past relationships.

People asked why we didn't touch or hold hands as they saw we definitely had eyes for each other. Even though he wanted to hold my hand, Lee had set the goal that if we were still together when I graduated high school, then we could do that. When other guys around me started wanting to hug me or pursue me, I'd tell them that I didn't even hug the guy I was in a relationship with. While I'm a very huggy person, it actually was nice to have an excuse as guys at school got more "feely" around different girls. I think some guys thought I was playing "hard to get" and tried harder to pursue me, but I definitely wasn't and had no intention of being disloyal. If anything, I thought Lee might be too good for me with his high standards that had now become my own.

While I had made up my mind to keep guys at a distance, my highly sensitive nature kept trying to make me think *this is the one. Lee respects me and is trying to protect my heart.* Any time I expressed how deeply I felt, he was sure to keep me "in check." I often wondered if he felt as deeply for me as I did him since he wasn't the most expressive guy, though very honorable. When an older friend flirted with him and kept trying to mediate between us despite me not wanting her to, it was hurtful.

When my sister, her husband, and I visited his house for a conference, we needed to stay in Lee's room. In it, we saw his book collection, including a journal that I just happened to pick up and open, reading his prayer to God that my heart would be protected and not hurt by his interactions with my friend. While curious, I didn't want to pry anymore. It was enough for me to know that Lee cared about my heart and was trying to protect me. I didn't even know I had a heart worth protecting at the time. Even more, the way he wrote to God calling him his Dad made me want that same kind of relationship for myself.

My relationship with my own dad was often very distant and hurtful. While I had diaries in the past, I had never really thought about journaling or writing to God on a regular basis. This one night where I stumbled upon Lee's journal to God probably affected me more than anything else in our entire relationship. While things didn't last between us, I look back during that time, the standards he helped me set, the way I learned my heart was worth protecting, and my newfound practice of journaling to God, and I am still so thankful.

During that time of journaling to God, I got closer than ever before to Him. I was once again reminded of the God who heard the little desire of my heart when I was only four years old. Only now, I had evidence of all the ways He spoke to me each and every day. I could see with my own eyes when God answered different prayers. When I struggled in faith for yet another prayer, I would look back on all the ways He was so faithful to me over the years. When my favorite grandma died, my sister and brother moved out that were closest to me, my cousin became paralyzed in a car accident, and a great uncle died in the same hospital all in the same month, He was the one to comfort my hurting heart. God was the one who cradled me and acted as a loving Father when my dad's anger surmounted with the different circumstances in our lives. I found a love and trust in this invisible Being I didn't know was possible or at least had forgotten was possible. I felt safe to open my heart to Him and started trusting that He would bring the right guy in the right timing.

When I did finally meet my husband, everything seemed far too good to be true (because it was). We had so many confirmations that God had brought us together, and I was thrilled that I could finally dive in and let my heart and emotions take over. When we first met, Drew cared for me, seemed head over heels in love with me, and shared such strong feelings that I once again allowed my heart to picture those rolling hills on the side of the roads with the love that would remain in my life. I let my heart dream again of a future of happiness—wild and free. Only this time, I was certain God was a part of it and led me there since we had so many confirmations.

As my relationship with Drew didn't at all look like the picture that I had in my mind and I felt far from being prized or valued with the different struggles he was facing, my trust in God's care became shattered as well. I no longer pictured those rolling hills with excitement or hope. I would look at them while driving, wishing I could jump out and escape, anywhere from my reality. I no longer pictured Heaven in the same way either because it would be surrounded by a God that I no longer knew cared for me.

As I was riding in our van on the way to my hometown and saw those rolling hills all over again, those visions flashed before my eyes, and tears started streaming down my face. I thought about my reality not looking or feeling like what I had envisioned. I tried to close my eyes and shut out those thoughts, but I felt a little nudge to look again. This time, I looked up at the most beautiful, dreamy sky and felt like maybe I could hope again. I pictured myself twirling in the grass with God shining upon me and looking down on me with delight and thought, *"It was always You. You were my first Love and my one great Love who delights in me."* As I started to weep and see the clouds floating in the peaceful sky, my favorite Scripture during my years of journaling came to mind: "Whom have I in heaven *but You?* And *there is* none upon earth *that* I desire besides You. My flesh and my heart fail; *But* God *is* the strength of my heart and my portion forever."[1]

As God started picking up and mending the pieces of my broken heart and sharing how greatly He cared for me in the midst of all the trials I had faced, God showed me how much He wanted to hold me in His arms during those times in a way I could feel it. He reminded me of the Love I had long since forgotten and what drew me to Him in the first place.

FIRST AND LAST

What happened to my Love,
Once held dear to my heart?
What happened to the days I vowed
We would never be apart?

How could I ever dare
To leave my best Friend,
The One Who'd always love me
Right to the very end?

What happened to my longing
To always be near You?
What happened to my desire
To let You choose what we'd do?

How can I prove to You
I couldn't have been more wrong?
How did I ever leave You?
Oh, it's been too long...

How are You doing?
How have You been?
Is there ever a chance
We could start all over again?

'Cause You were my first Love
And I want You to be my last
Can we forget what was between us?
Can we put it in the past?

I know I was the one to leave You
You don't have to come back to me
I'm sorry I let things come between us
But please accept my apology

And yet You've been constantly waiting
For me to find
You never stopped loving me
I never left Your mind

Oh Lord, I don't deserve You
I could never repay
I don't deserve Your light, Your love
That's with me every day

So I'm not gonna let things come between us
Like I did in the past
'Cause You were my first Love, Jesus
And will be my last

Reflect:

HAVE you accepted God's love for you? If not, why not? Dig deep. While feelings feel so big and emotional and out of our control, there's always a reason behind them. Don't be afraid to explore that side of you.

THINK BACK on a time when you felt God so close. Now, how about a time you felt He was so far away? What changed in those circumstances?

I'D ENCOURAGE you to not only pray about those times but also write in a journal to Him. God is a God who can be trusted—a faithful Love to the end. As you journal to Him, I know you'll see that as well.

Write a love note to God. It might feel awkward at first, but a journal to God rather than a diary was always one of the most comforting notebooks I kept as a teen. I highly recommend it.

Don't forget to date it and even sign it like you would a love letter. It's such an awesome thing to be able to go back and look upon old entries and see God move when you just simply decide to choose Him. If you don't have a good one, you can still write in any old notebook for now. However, I'd encourage you to buy a good one that you'll enjoy writing in when you get the chance. You can even transfer your note into the new one for a nice start.

God desires for us to know how much He loves us, how He's always been there for us, and desires to be chosen and loved just like we do. When the going gets tough, He hopes that we'll go all in and be fully committed just like He is.

9

COMMIT

"Commit your works to the LORD,
And your thoughts will be established."
Proverbs 16:3 (NKJV)

The Lord says: "These people come near to Me with their mouth and honor Me with their lips, but their hearts are far from Me. Their worship of Me is based on merely human rules they have been taught."
Isaiah 29:13 (NIV)

"If you don't plan to live the Christian life totally committed to knowing your God and to walking in obedience to Him, then don't begin; for this is what Christianity is all about. It is a change of citizenship, a change of governments, a change of allegiance. If you have no intention of letting Christ rule your life, then forget Christianity; it's not for you."

Kay Arthur

The first six years or so of my marriage were so incredibly hard. There was so much hurt and deception early on that I often wondered if I made a bad choice. While there's a part of me that believes that once you marry someone, they inevitably become "the one," the amount of deception involved often made me feel like I never truly had a choice in the matter. As a result, I toyed with the idea that maybe I married the "wrong one" and the "right one" was still out there. It left room for sick games to be played in my mind.

When things got really bad, I'd find my mind trying to escape to this imaginary world where I still had the excitement of anticipation that I might still be wanted and pursued by some unknown lover or a friend from my past I deeply cared about but thought was too good for me. I'd quickly shut down those fantasies in an effort to keep my mind pure, but it was a constant struggle for me.

For most of my life, I didn't struggle at all with those kinds of thoughts. I wasn't one to read romance novels, I tried to filter what I allowed into my mind, and I didn't entertain any unrealistic dreams. The furthest I had gone with anyone before my husband was holding hands and an occasional hug. I sought purity through and through. I didn't quite understand why it was after marriage that I struggled the most. It wasn't that I was trying to go to those places in my mind. If anything, as soon as I had those thoughts, I automatically felt guilty and ashamed for them because of my long-held beliefs about marriage, infidelity starting in the mind, and my spouse becoming "the one" as soon as I said, "I do."

Yet, even with my guard up, it was a constant struggle. It baffled me that it was becoming such a stronghold in my life as it wasn't anything I'd feel in the slightest bit comfortable acting upon. I even took it a step further by trying to bring rationality into my thoughts. I realized that even if someone were wanting to pursue me while I was married, he wouldn't be the good man I thought he was—as someone who is willing to cheat with you is willing to cheat on you. If I were to engage in anything physically or mentally outside of my marriage, I'd just be building another relationship not founded upon trust. No matter how I looked at it, it wasn't something I truly wanted no matter how much my mind kept trying to escape to that place.

It wasn't until I read a book called "Boundaries" by Dr. Henry Cloud and Dr. John Townsend that it became less of a struggle for me. At that point in my life, my husband was still in a very untrustworthy season in our marriage. How I discovered that felt like another slap in the face and left me wondering if it was even possible to have a good relationship with him or if I even wanted to stick around and try. With how much of a struggle it was to not create a fantasy escape in my mind before then, I would have thought it would have been an even greater struggle with my newfound revelation. Yet, after reading the book, the desire to escape was almost nonexistent. If I did have those thoughts, I was able to finally quickly shut them down without the same struggle I had dealt with before.

You see, at that point, I felt like I had really good excuses to divorce my husband. In fact, I had built up enough courage to face the shame of it and had every intention to act upon it. I felt that if people knew what was going on, they would have agreed with me. Yet, the very day I had made up my mind to do it, God shared His plan with me through the mouth of an old friend and marriage counselor. God spoke His vision for our marriage through her words and broke down the walls of rightness and victimhood I had been building into our marriage—the thoughts that said I didn't have a choice in the matter. In fact, it was the first time in our married life I actually felt like I did.

As I mentioned before, our circumstances made me feel that I had no choice in our relationship. As a result, I started playing a victim in my mind and made my husband out to be the bad guy. While my husband made a lot of stupid choices, he wasn't the enemy I made him out to be and I wasn't the victim I had been playing out either. I had every choice whether I stayed in the relationship or not and what hand I'd play in it from then on. While I couldn't make his choices for him or stop his actions, I could control the way in which I responded. I could decide If I was willing to stay in the relationship and whether or not I could choose to love a fallen man.

With my newfound vision for our marriage and a growing knowledge of boundaries, I lovingly but firmly told my husband I had no intention of ever divorcing him, but I also couldn't afford for our kids to see me in a constant roller coaster of emotions over things that didn't even pertain to them. If I needed to, I would take the time away to separate myself from him and get the healing I needed. It was somewhat of a wakeup call for him. While that certainly wasn't the end of our struggles, it was one of the first times I felt like I was powerful enough to direct our fate. With the hope that God wasn't finished with our story and was going to use our struggles to help others, I made the choice that I was going to stay and be fully committed to our relationship. When I willfully chose to commit, it left no room for any outside doubts or fantasies to creep in and gave me the power to back up my choice.

Just as we must not leave ourselves empty and must fill up and choose, we have to decide whether we are going to be fully committed in our relationship to God—just as I had to choose to make the commitment to my husband. As soon as I felt like I had a choice in the matter and made that choice to be all in it, I was no longer seeking an escape. To leave any room for doubt or indecisiveness allows our enemy to wreak havoc in our minds. There's a reason God commands us to love Him with all our heart, soul, mind, and strength.[1] He knows if we leave any space in our lives vacant, it leaves us susceptible to an enemy trying to occupy our minds. It wouldn't take long for him to try to steal our attention, hearts, and very lives.

God is an all-or-nothing God. He would rather us be cold or hot than lukewarm. Christ wants a pure bride who wants Him and wholly Him. God doesn't want us to feel like we've settled and dabble with thoughts of lust for His enemy. As an all-consuming fire and a jealous God, He wants to be wanted all for Himself—not sharing us with lesser gods and idols we've made for ourselves. He either wants all of us or nothing at all.

ALL OR NOTHING

I speak of trusting You
I speak of making a difference
But every opportunity You put me through
I'm afraid to cross the fence

I need to swallow my pride
Exalt Your name on high
Never bring it to shame
'Cause it's all or nothing . . .
And nothing's not why You came

I'm tired of giving You some
I'm desperate to give You all
I'm tired of being a spiritual bum
Who doesn't answer to Your call

Forgive me for my weakness
Strengthen me by Your right hand
Oh Lord, give me meekness
Help me conquer this land

Because to know You
Is to make You known
And the least I can do
Is let Your light be shone

So help me swallow my pride
Exalt Your name on high
Never bring it to shame
'Cause it's all or nothing . . .
And nothing's not why You came

GOD WANTS us to come to a place where we won't ever desire another lesser lover. He wants us to fall head over heels in love with Him and be ruined for another. When we choose and commit to Him wholeheartedly, God will show us He's far greater than we could ever wish He'd be and faithful even when we stray.

RUINED

Look what I do to You.
What I continue to do to You.
I run away from You, my Love . . .
And You promise to never leave.
I'm so good at portraying a harlot.
I'm so good at loving little gods more than You.

I'm so good at turning my back on You after
swearing I'd never leave.
And I'm tired of running from You.
I'm tired of trying to escape this kind
of love 'cause I'm scared.
I'm tired of being scared of experiencing a love like this.
Maybe I've never known what true love is before . . .
But You continue to show it to me.
I've never known what beauty is until I saw
Your valuable sacrifice.
Why would You do this for me?
I'm so undeserving.
I don't mean to say that Your creation isn't great,
But I'm definitely not what I should be.
I wasn't made to be this way.
I was made to be the clay that You shape.
Why do I run away from You, Potter, when
I wish to be
the way You wish to make me?
It all comes so naturally,
Running away from You like I do.
Why? Why don't I just stay where I belong and let You finish
Your sculpting?
I'm good at causing ruin.
Am I a ruin?
Are You going to give up on me?
I wouldn't blame You.
But just when I think You're going to give up on me,
You put me through the flames, the sweltering heat.
But only because You love me.
I wouldn't be everything I was created to be
without those flames.
And now You're trying to brand me with Your name.
"You're mine. Forever and always, Jesus."

Why do You love me so?
Why don't You just give up on me like I deserve?
Why do You make me so fearfully and wonderfully made?
I am a ruin . . . I'm ruined by Your love
because I can never repay.
When I found the One my soul loves, I held Him
and would not let Him go.
I love You, Jesus.
I'm never letting You go.
No, no . . . I'm ruined by Your love.

(Sentence in italics from Song of Solomon 3:4)

Reflect:

HAVE you fully committed yourself to Christ? If not, what's stopping you?

AFTER YOU'VE MADE the commitment to Christ, I'd encourage you to get baptized if you haven't been already. Baptism is an external action to show one's internal commitment. Think of it as the engagement or marriage ceremony letting others know you've made the commitment to give your life to Him.

If you've been baptized and don't feel the need to be baptized again but want to rededicate your life to Him, don't be afraid to go to an altar to show your commitment externally or ask for accountability from someone who inspires you in your walk. There's power in outward obedience and actions, and in letting others know your intentions.

Be forewarned though, it was after Jesus was baptized that He was led into the wilderness to be tempted by the devil.[2] It seems that after we've made the commitment to choose Christ, Satan starts to see the potential for us to be a threat, and we need to prepare ourselves.

PREPARE YOURSELF

"Now prepare yourself like a man;
I will question you, and you shall answer Me."
Job 38:3 (NKJV)

"Stay alert! Watch out for your great enemy, the devil. He
prowls around like a roaring lion, looking
for someone to devour."
1 Peter 5:8 (NLT)

"Spiritual warfare is very real. There is a furious, fierce, and ferocious battle raging in the realm of the spirit between the forces of God and the forces of evil. Warfare happens every day, all the time. Whether you believe it or not, you are in a battlefield. You are in warfare."
Pedro Okoro

*A*s a sixteen-year-old, I wasn't one to easily scare. Yet, there I was hiding underneath my blanket like a young, frightened child—terrified to even look out my window. My small twin bed lay just to the left of it, and I had the strongest sense someone was watching me through it. I couldn't shake the feeling no matter how hard I tried. I attempted to turn my head away—my closed eyes facing the opposing wall in prayer, only to visualize a multitude of gruesome creatures I had never seen before. As I lay there, I pulled the covers up over my head, got into a ball, and continued praying fervently in the Spirit for what felt like a good hour before these terrifying creatures disappeared and I could finally fall asleep in peace.

I was awoken early the next morning by my dad asking me if I had gotten home late and couldn't get into our house. "No . . . why?" I asked. He told me that one of the chairs was taken off our front porch, and he found it right underneath my unlocked window.

It was then that I realized there was a reason for what I'd been feeling. I've often wondered who was there, what intentions they had, and what happened to stop them from attempting to get in. I've wondered if I felt the person's "aura" or if it was just the Holy Spirit prompting me to pray. There's no question in my mind that something was going on in the spirit realm that night.

THE NEXT TIME I had that strong sense and visualized such demonic creatures was not long after my husband and I got married. Thankfully it didn't last nearly as long, and I wasn't alone in my room. My husband and I were both lying in bed. He had fallen asleep, but I tapped him on his shoulder to ask him if he could pray with me. I was frightened again—not being able to shake the feeling or visions I'd seen—and told him the story of the last time I felt that way. He said a quick prayer, told me everything would be ok, and turned to go back to sleep. I tried to sleep, but I couldn't ignore the images in my mind or the uneasy feeling growing in the pit of my stomach. I told him I still didn't feel at peace and asked him to pray again with me. I rarely kept him awake in those days, and he knew I wouldn't let him go back to sleep in such a state, so he begrudgingly turned over and prayed once again with me, reassuring me everything was going to be ok.

The next morning, my husband opened the adjoining door from our house into our garage only to find it unlocked. He'd accidentally left the garage door open overnight, and both of our bikes had been stolen. We lived in a decent, small-town neighborhood in northern Indiana and didn't even know of anybody who had had that happen to them. While we usually shut our garage door and locked up every night, getting our bikes stolen wasn't something that had ever crossed our mind to even watch out for. However, we realized then that we should pay attention when I have such strong feelings, be prepared to pray fervently in the spirit, and be ready to fight.

WHILE I WISH I could say I've always remained alert and in tune with the spirit realm, I haven't. I could see some of the smaller battles for what they were, but I didn't prepare myself for the season I was about to be in. The wilderness season I went through was like a chronic disease that constantly chipped away at the life I once knew and caused me to take on the stance of a victim. I didn't see it for what it was. Instead of resisting the devil, I resisted the season I was in, the people I felt perpetuated it, and the God who led me there.

At the time, I didn't see that God had led me into this wilderness season because He loved me. It was like the onset of the story of Job I wanted to skim over and pretend didn't happen. The parts where Satan comes to present himself before God, saying he's been roaming back and forth throughout the earth, only for God to point out Job—not once but twice—bragging on him and holding up his integrity like tasty bait for a ferocious predator. It's this wild part of God's personality that David talks about in Psalm 23:5 when he says that God prepares a table before him in the presence of his enemies. It's God's uninhibited way of showing off His beloved ones, fully knowing what it means we will be up against. In a surprising manner, it's the process He allows to discipline us. It's His way of expressing His love for us and belief in us. Like a father who loves His children, God disciplines those He loves and in doing so, shows we are His legitimate children. He knows that in the end, it will produce a harvest of righteousness and peace that we all seek to possess.[1]

Instead of "counting it all joy" when that happens like we're instructed to in James 1:2, we often ask, "How could a loving God allow someone He loves and believes in to go through such pain?" We don't want to see that God did that to Jesus, Daniel, Job, Joseph, David, and basically all the people He used mightily. We don't want to acknowledge that even Jesus learned obedience through His sufferings.[2] We don't want to surrender our lives and say "Not my will, but Yours be done" as Jesus did. In our pride, we ask Him, "Why me?" rather than "Why not me?" as though something we've done or could do might stop the mighty will of God and the overwhelming hatred His enemy has for those who bear His image. We want the testimony without the test, but that's not how God works.

After several years of trial upon trial and the most deafening silence I had ever experienced, I thought God had given up on me. I didn't think He believed in me anymore. I didn't believe in myself anymore. I was stripped of everything I once held dear. I gave up the hope that I alone had anything to offer. I didn't realize that was right where He wanted me. I didn't realize that the test was meant to humble me. God led me in that season and held back His presence to prepare me for what was to come in my life. He didn't want me to rely on my own strength anymore, as that was very limited. He wanted the faulty foundations I built my life upon to crumble so that I would surrender my life, depend on Him, and lean on His stability.

STABILITY

Everything's running along
Nothing can go wrong
But then a huge turn
A new lesson you gotta learn

You think you let go
Let God run the show
Slowly emotions coming back
When will you get cut some slack?

Your spirit's warring inside
You wanna scream, you wanna hide
Find it's all a dream
With you on the winning team

Oh, if life were that easy
If emotions were so breezy
Maybe hearts would never be broken
Maybe pain would never be awoken

But we have to face reality

Stop living in a fantasy
Of a world that's never changing
Of a heart needing no re-arranging

But child, when the pain gets to you
When everything turns and you don't know what to do
Turn to Me, I'm able
The only thing that will always remain stable

Wanna be there through it all
Wanna catch you when you fall
Just let go, you have the ability
Let Me be your stability

JUST LIKE JOB had to endure a horrific time of affliction, just like Joseph had to go through a time of false accusation and trials, and just like Jesus was led into the wilderness, it seems that God often leads us into a wilderness season "to be tempted by the devil" just as Jesus was. When we make that public commitment to pledge our lives to God, we are now seen as a threat. Satan wants us to forget our purpose and who we are, and God allows that time to empty us of ourselves, take on a partnership with Him, and strengthen and prepare us for the future plans He has for us.

When we see those trials for what they are—not a result of punishment, but rather because He loves us—we can learn to consider them with joy knowing that if we persevere when our faith is tried, they will produce a maturity in us that will be perfect and complete, lacking nothing as James 2:1-4 shares. It is when we are vigilant and prepare ourselves as a soldier ready for battle rather than taking a stance as a victim, we can see those trials as the training ground they were always meant to be.

Instead of being on the defensive, we can learn to fight back and become the threat God created us to be and Satan feared we might become.

Reflect:

THINK of a time that you were in a difficult season, what were the things you questioned about God? About yourself?

DO you feel like that time brought you closer to God or further away from Him? Why?

WHEN YOU WERE GOING through that difficult time, did you see it as punishment or love?

WHAT DOES that tell you about your beliefs?

ARE there any truths to combat the lies you believed during that time?

NOW THAT I discussed the imperative need to prepare ourselves for battle, I'll share how we can fight back.

FIGHT BACK

"If you fight back and get hit, it hurts a little while; if you don't fight back, it hurts forever."
Joel Siegel

"For the weapons of our warfare *are* not carnal but mighty in God for pulling down strongholds, casting down arguments and every high thing that exalts itself against the knowledge of God, bringing every thought into captivity to the obedience of Christ, and being ready to punish all disobedience when your obedience is fulfilled."
2 Corinthians 10:4-6 (NKJV)

"Submit yourselves, then, to God. Resist the devil, and he will flee from you."
James 4:7 (NIV)

"You can't steal my joy, Satan! You can't steal my joy!" I desperately shouted in the cold silence driving back home late at night from work. Tears were streaming down my face as I replayed all the happenings of that evening. My very first night of my first real job besides babysitting, and I was robbed of $600. Apparently, the thievery was going on for some time before I arrived, but I was an easy target. The rest of the night at work was spent talking to security and filing a report in my small parking garage booth before I finally headed home. When I was alone in my car, I let out my frustrations and hurt. I think it was the first time I ever talked to Satan out loud. I couldn't tell you if it was my last, but these days, I'd like to think I've matured some in my approach.

For most of my life, I've been hyper aware of the unseen. From being healed of a broken collarbone, to prayers answered and words of knowledge given that only God could have known, to these awful feelings I just couldn't shake—there have been times in my life I wished that I wasn't so aware. I wished I could disregard it or live in ignorant bliss as others seem to.

I've realized that when it comes to the spiritual realm, most people either seem to ignore it, fear it, demonize it, or even overly spiritualize it to the point that they completely neglect the physical realm. Just as God is three-in-one, we each contain three parts as well—body, soul, and spirit. It's so easy to neglect one or compartmentalize rather than treating them all as a whole. However, when one part suffers, the rest suffer too. It seems so many completely neglect their spiritual lives not realizing just how much it's affecting every other part of their lives as well.

I haphazardly tried that when I felt God didn't care for me. I worked so hard to box up my feelings and live a numb existence. I attempted to live just under the radar. I didn't want to be seen as a threat, but I also couldn't muster up the passion to go all in anymore. When I was in that place, even after coming back from a suicide attempt, I often felt like a traitor. Over and over again, no matter how hard I'd try to please God, I felt like I was coming up short. I had such a hard time believing that God could use me anymore. I felt too far gone, too much of a failure to be of use. I thought God must be punishing me and that He must not love me.

Similar to Jesus' temptations, Satan got me questioning if I was a Christian anymore after all. He even used Scripture just as He did with Jesus. The verses that were replayed over and over again in my mind were Hebrews 6:4-6 (NIV):

> It is impossible for those who have once been enlightened, who have tasted the heavenly gift, who have shared in the Holy Spirit, who have tasted the goodness of the word of God and the powers of the coming age and who have fallen away, to be brought back to repentance. To their loss they are crucifying the Son of God all over again and subjecting Him to public disgrace.

While those verses are in Scripture, I began to realize that Scripture is never meant to be used against people, including myself. That's what Satan did to Jesus when he tempted Him. Jesus isn't an accuser of the brethren; Satan is.[1] While I didn't have the power to save myself, I took into account what was said in Mark 10:27 (ESV): "Jesus looked at them and said, 'With man it is impossible, but not with God. For all things are possible with God.'" Then I reminded myself, and even spoke over myself looking in the mirror at times, "I can do all things through Christ who gives me strength."[2]

I reminded myself that Proverbs 24:16 says, "Though a righteous man falls seven times, he will rise again, but the wicked will fall by calamity." Some translations say he *may* fall, while others profess with absolute certainty that he will. The only difference between the righteous and the wicked falling it would seem is that the righteous will get back up again.

WARRIOR

Don't doubt my strength
I know I may be a girl
But underneath me is a warrior
Just waiting to be revealed
The time will come
When you will see
All His strength
Inside of me
Just be patient
Don't give up on me
I know I may fall down
But I'll always get back up
For deep inside of me
I have a Strength
Way greater than me
Just waiting to be revealed

JUST LIKE HE did to Jesus, Satan always seems to start out with "if you're really the daughter of God . . . " and tries to get us to question our identity, our relationship to the Father, and ultimately, our worth. If he can make us forget those things, he knows that our purpose will be thwarted in the process.

If we're not prepared or expecting him, he knows we won't fight back. We'll just accept his voice as our own or those he uses against us instead of resisting him. When we don't submit to

God and His voice or resist the devil, we give this master manipulator permission to stay there and torture us with his lies and bully ourselves rather than making him flee.

When that wilderness season comes upon us or we've already been through it but feel like we've failed, we need to remind Satan and ourselves who we are, Whose we are, and that God has our backs. Nothing is impossible for Him. When all is said and done, we know who wins in the end. When we partner with God, we will be victorious also.

GOD HAS WON THE VICTORY

A warrior I once was,
Bent knees,
Tear-stained cheeks,
Fighting off the enemy

I don't know when I forgot where I was
When this battlefield started feeling safe
When our unrelenting enemy got me to sit back
Take off my armor, not retaliate

I don't know when I tuned Your orders out
I don't know why I tried to take command
I don't know how to give this battle to You
I wish I could put it back into Your hands

I've been taken prisoner now
The enemy's yelling in my face
He's calling me, wanting me to be a traitor
Wants me to believe I've fallen from grace

I don't want to believe him

But part of me still does
But with my last breath of hope
I cry out, "Jesus!"

The enemy shudders
As You come on the scene
All his demonic troops have left him
Your presence makes them flee

The enemy starts accusing me
Spitting in my face
Silenced by Your scars
You remind him, "I've already taken her place"

Tears are shed, the battle's won
As our enemy leaves the scene
And once again, I can proclaim,
"God has won the victory!"

Reflect:

1 Peter 4:12-13 says, "Beloved, do not think it strange concerning the fiery trial which is to try you, as though some strange thing happened to you; but rejoice to the extent that you partake of Christ's sufferings, that when His glory is revealed, you may also be glad with exceeding joy."

When you were being tried in the past, did you ever stop to ask which spirit was speaking over you?

. . .

WERE your thoughts uplifting and encouraging, or were they condemning and accusing?

WHICH WAY DOES SATAN SPEAK? Which way does Christ speak?

WHOSE WORDS WERE you believing and speaking over yourself? How can you improve?
1 John 4:1-6 says this:

> Beloved, do not believe every spirit, but test the spirits, whether they are of God; because many false prophets have gone out into the world. By this you know the Spirit of God: Every spirit that confesses that Jesus Christ has come in the flesh is of God, and every spirit that does not confess that Jesus Christ has come in the flesh is not of God. And this is the *spirit* of the Antichrist, which you have heard was coming, and is now already in the world. You are of God, little children, and have overcome them, because He who is in you is greater than he who is in the world. They are of the world. Therefore they speak *as* of the world, and the world hears them. We are of God. He who knows God hears us; he who is not of God does not hear us. By this we know the spirit of truth and the spirit of error.

So often it seems that we use these verses to condemn others and tell them not to believe people we deem to be false prophets. However, through this journey, I've found that I have been the one believing spirits who have falsely prophesied over myself and others before their time. When I judge others, I condemn myself.[3] When I speak evil and accuse others God put in authority, I can't possibly know where they're at on their own journey. Even angels, who are greater in might and power than me, wouldn't dare to do the same.[4]

ROMANS 8:1-2 SAYS: "Therefore, there is now no condemnation for those who are in Christ Jesus. For in Christ Jesus the law of the Spirit of life set you free from the law of sin and death."

If your thoughts are condemning you, resist them. Satan doesn't make his appearance obvious. The battlefield is for our minds. We don't fight against flesh and blood.[5] Test what spirit is speaking to you—over yourself and others. God isn't an accuser of the brethren, Satan is.

When accusatory and condemning thoughts enter your mind, remind yourself that's how the enemy approaches us. He starts by casting doubt and says, "*If* you really are a son or daughter of God . . . " However, Jesus seems to approach us with a reminder of who He is and who we are in Him. He starts out with affirming our identity by calling us "Beloved" and continues with "You are of God, little children..."

We are to cast down every argument and every high thing that exalts itself against the knowledge of God and bring every thought into captivity to the obedience of Christ.[6]

In the next chapter, I will talk about the Spirit of life that Christ offers us that sets us free from the law of sin and death. I hope it frees our spirits from the condemnation Satan tries to get us to take upon ourselves, helps us continually resist him, and walk in the possibilities God has for us all.

SECTION IV

POSSIBILITY

FREE YOUR SPIRIT

"It is for freedom that Christ has set us free. Stand firm, then,
and do not let yourselves be burdened
again by a yoke of slavery."
Galatians 5:1 (NIV)

"By realizing the reality of our Prince within us, we are never bothered again by the fact that we do not understand ourselves, or that other people do not understand us. The only One who truly understands me is the One who made me and redeems me…. It is a tremendous freedom to get rid of every kind of self-consideration and learn to care about only one thing- the relationship between our Prince and ourselves."
Oswald Chambers

I used to listen to and read music lyrics so often and so intently when I was younger, I could have probably pursued a job in it. When my parents were working and my older siblings were busy, VH1's music videos like Jewel's "Foolish Games," R.E.M.'s "Losing My Religion" (At the time, it was the only music video sung live on set and I thought that was so cool.), The Cranberries' "Zombie," or anything by Goo Goo Dolls or Matchbox Twenty gave me life. Music was my medicine of choice to numb any pain I experienced in life.

When I got filled with the Holy Spirit at twelve, I still loved all those bands, but I'd occasionally change the lyrics. Vertical Horizon's "Everything You Want" lyrics became "God's everything you want, everything you need, God's everything inside of you that you wish you could be." Over time and discovery and introduction from close friends, I gradually started enjoying more Christian bands that weren't as well-known at the time. I didn't have to change a lot of lyrics then. It didn't bother me in the least when other friends still liked the songs I had previously enjoyed. However, on my own, I made a conscious decision that I wanted to fill my mind with good things that kept my focus on God.

Four years into my new lifestyle, I went to a women's retreat where one of the pastor's daughters was sharing how she told her mom she had decided to listen to only Christian music and her mom was so proud of her—it deepened their relationship with each other. Knowing my own lack in my relationship, how we butted heads, and how I sought her pride, I shared with her that four years ago I had made the same choice. Only, I wasn't met with pride or joy. I was met with a reprimand that I had ever listened to secular music in the first place. All my CDs were ransacked, and my new Relient K disc I had just bought for $16 with babysitting money was thrown into the trash for not being "Christian enough." I was devastated. There was a part of me that became fearful of ever becoming like that, and another part of me that was determined not to open up to my mom again. When my red 1987 Nissan Pulsar's radio decided the only station that would come in clearly was Delilah's light rock 105.7, I welcomed it. In a way, I felt a little bit of shame, but the other part of me was glad for the excuse.

It started a cycle in my spirit that had a hard time separating shame from freedom. I still listened to Christian music on my own when there was a choice and found a lot of comfort and joy in various songs and lyrics, but part of me no longer felt like there really was a choice if I wanted to please God and my parents. It felt like duty and obligation rather than a choice made from freedom and love.

THE LION IN THE LAMB

I see you looking at me
Your eyes gazing so pitifully
My once piercing eyes
Have been replaced with a lifeless stare
And I'm aching to be anywhere
But here

You were once in awe of me
Full of life, running wild
Yet you feared what I could be
As an untamed child
Now you're painfully aware
Of what you made of me

My fearless roam
Has been replaced
With steps in a line

And a steady pace
Yet I feel so out of place
Following in your footsteps

You've always thought I was too free-spirited
So I've always been somewhat berated
For dancing to a drum
You never heard of
When all I've ever wanted
Was to be truly loved
For who I am

But I fear until the end of my age
I'll always remain
A lion in a cage
Unless you unleash all that I am
And let me be
The lion in the lamb

(My name, Rachel, means "Little Lamb.")

I WAS ALREADY LAX in my judgment of others that pinned me as a "free spirit," but part of me started resonating more with those outside of the Christian box I was in. The reason I had always loved Goo Goo Dolls, Matchbox Twenty, or Train was not only for their musical ability and sound, but because they sang of imperfect girls like me who they seemed to love perfectly. The women's flaws only seemed to enhance their beauty, and their complexities gave them depth. I never seemed to measure up to the standards set in my life, despite being a type one on the Enneagram and seeking excellence as I tried to be "above reproach" in everything I did. I always felt like I was too much or not enough. It didn't help that I'm an INFJ that often stood out from the crowd and never really felt like I truly fit into any circle I was in. It also wasn't great that other parents would joke that they wanted to adopt me because I was a positive role model for their kids, but I was told, "It's because they don't know or live with you." I wanted so badly to be loved for everything I was and everything I encompassed, but I felt a part of me had to be hidden. I felt like something deep in my core must be wrong with me. Though I was often pegged as too transparent and often told I was sharing too much information, a part of me felt the need to keep myself at a distance.

I felt like no one could truly love me if they knew everything about me—except God, my sister who believed the best about me, and my gracious best friend who had her own struggles with religion. However, my sister moved a few states away at sixteen, and my friend's schedule often didn't line up with my own. God was truly the only one I felt free to be myself with. He was the One who cared enough to answer the desires of my heart from a young age before I knew right from wrong. He was the One who broke down the walls of any box I or anyone else ever tried to put Him in. God was the One who spoke to me and comforted me no matter the circumstance I was in. He gave me strength when I got robbed the first night of my first job, and He comforted me when fear and hurt caused a loved one to unleash pent up anger on me and become someone I no longer knew. God knew me—my fears, likes, hurt, anger, and dreams—and loved me enough to stick around. I felt free to be myself with Him. Best of all, I actually felt like He liked me—even with all my idiosyncrasies and imperfections.

There's this ugly root that springs up from religion. It starts out seemingly innocent and often out of a pure desire to please God. It gets some foundational truths right, but somewhere along the way, it gets caught up in fear and causes those immersed in it to become stuck. It opens the door to a spirit that causes all those who follow it to lose their ability to operate in power, love, and a sound mind. Even worse, it speaks evil of the power that comes from following God and walking closely with Him, masking itself as wisdom and carefulness that is foolish to God.[1]

It speaks of the wisdom that comes from fearing God, but it misses the next step where God says that perfect love casts out fear and all the times He shares how much He loves us perfectly. It speaks truth of our deceitful hearts,[2] but it fails to mention that God promises He will give us a new heart and put a new spirit within us.[3] It likes to call us sinners, but it wouldn't dare call us saints, although it's mentioned 229 times in the Bible. It delights in false humility and regulations and shames freedom or anyone who walks in it.[4]

Many immersed in religion like to talk about what will come upon those who add onto the Bible, but they often miss the danger in those who take away from it.[5] Religion likes to condemn the "prosperity gospel," yet seems to hide the truth in Psalm 1 that says that whatever the godly man does shall prosper and over 100 other verses talking about God's blessing of prosperity for the godly. It likes to speak blessings on those who are poor and cuts out the rest that says, "in spirit."

I could go on and on. However, the worst part about it is that it puts God in a box that can fit in one's hands all in the name of not adding or taking away from it. It stuffs all His followers in along with Him and limits the faith of possibilities. It speaks of Jesus being the truth and the Word, yet it stops short of His very heart and Spirit and the glorious gospel, freedom, and life that have been made available to us. It wants us to believe that the same Holy Spirit that lives inside of Jesus doesn't live inside of us. It glorifies Jesus as the One, but it forgets to mention He's the firstborn among many brothers and sisters. It wants to keep half of the human race silent and in submission to the other half—dependent on the other. It overlooks the part where God says to submit to one another or that the Holy Spirit teaches us all things—as though the Holy Spirit isn't made available to women.

J.S. Park accurately described those of us dealing with a religious spirit:

> I meet Christians who are super-glossy, picture-perfect, law-abiding people, but they are absolutely miserable and difficult to be near. Their every movement is dictated by a strict rigid ruleset that is motivated by a desperate fear. If your efforts are not driven by grace—that God absolutely loves you no matter what—then you will punish yourself towards an invisible standard that looks like success but feels like slavery. Such a standard might work for a little while to conform your behavior, but it will never become a part of you: it's just an apparatus that imprisons you. Only grace can truly be internalized to melt your heart, and though it can take longer, a truly tenderized heart follows God with all joy and perseverance. This is motivation by grace and grace alone.

I've found that if Satan can't get us to walk into the trap of sin, he'll get us to walk into the silent and dangerous bondage of religion, trading the shackles of sin for the shackles of religion. What's worse is that religion is so much more engulfing and carries with it the heaviness of shame that is so incredibly hard to escape from. I know because I've been there. Park's quote I shared has described me at various points of my life. I'm still trying to cut off the chains I've allowed to ensnare me, reaching out to the glorious freedom Christ has laid out, paved the way, and made possible for me and you. This book is the evidence of that journey. I hope to share in the glorious freedom Christ has made possible by His Spirit.

So many get caught up in the Bible being the Word, yet they read it with a veil over their hearts,[6] unable to accept the things of the Spirit.[7] There's this great fear of anything New Age that condemns those who are "free-spirited," yet God's spirit brings freedom.

John 1:1 (emphasis mine) says, "In the beginning *was* the Word, and the Word *was* with God, and the Word *was* God."

John 1:14 (emphasis mine) goes on to say, "The Word *became* flesh and made His dwelling among us. We have seen His glory, the glory of the one and only Son, who came from the Father, full of grace and truth."

2 Corinthians 3:17-18 (emphasis mine) says, "***Now*** the Lord *is* the Spirit, and where the Spirit of the Lord *is*, there *is* freedom. And we all, who with unveiled faces contemplate the Lord's glory, ***are being*** transformed into His image with ever-increasing glory, which comes from the Lord, who *is* the Spirit."

The Bible doesn't make mistakes. It's inerrant. There was no mistake made with the verb tenses used. So many are reading Scripture thinking it's the end-all, be-all—condemning anyone who might say otherwise—but it was never meant to be an end unto itself. It's why the scribes and Pharisees, the very ones who had whole books of the Bible memorized and tried to follow the letter of the law to a "T," missed Jesus when He came. It's why those following in their footsteps still miss Him and the abundant life He offers now. Religion is the silent but deadly evil that chokes the life out of everything it touches and turns it into something it isn't—the leaven Jesus warned about (Krockett, K).

Jesus said in John 5:39-40 NKJV, "You search the Scriptures, for in them you think you have eternal life; and these are they which testify of Me. But you are not willing to come to Me that you may have life."

All Jesus did, will, and continues to do cannot be contained in Scriptures. John 21:25 says, "Jesus did many other things as well. If every one of them were written down, I suppose that even the whole world would not have room for the books that would be written."

God is the same God today that He was yesterday and forever will be.[8] He doesn't change.[9] He is still at work in the lives of His people. He is still a God of miracles and transformation. Even now, He is in the business of restoration and making all things new.[10]

Charles Spurgeon shared the following:

> When people hear about what God used to do, one of the things they say is: "Oh, that was a very long while ago." . . . I thought it was God that did it. Has God changed? Is He not an immutable God, the same yesterday, today and forever? Does not that furnish an argument to prove that what God has done at one time He can do at another? Nay, I think I may push it a little further, and say what He has done once, is a prophecy of what He intends to do again . . . whatever God has done . . . is to be looked upon as a precedent . . . [Let us] with earnestness seek that God would restore to us the faith of the men of old, that we may richly enjoy His grace as in the days of old.

Often, I'd read about Jesus being tempted in the wilderness and think how in the world did Satan show Him in an instant all the kingdoms of the world or lead Him to Jerusalem to stand on the highest point of the temple. Frequently, I'd overlook the fact that it was in the power of the Spirit or all the times it fell on Ezekiel, Saul, Samson, John, or Peter who fell into different trances (*Thirteen Verses about Trances*). When God started breaking the chains in my life, I was led in the power of the Spirit and it was as though I was looking at all the instances of my life from His viewpoint rather than my own. I never felt more loved than I had then. I never saw more purpose for everything I had gone through—good and bad—than I had at that moment. It and everything else made sense with such overwhelming clarity. When I got out of that experience and had to see what was possible and how to get there, my reality didn't line up at all with the visions I had or the rejection I would face. I realized I needed God's Spirit and grace to help me walk it out. It was the first time my strong-willed, independent self felt the need to truly surrender, knowing I couldn't walk this out on my own, yet also realizing the trust I would need to walk into the unknown.

When we break free from the shackles of religion and seek to follow His Spirit, we have to realize that our journey might look different from others. When we try to keep things exactly the way we think they should be or look like or try to limit our experience to stories and people we've read about in the Bible, we often block out what the Spirit is trying to do in and through us now.

The thing about a spirit is, it cannot be contained. Spirits aren't limited by time, space, or matter. They don't dwell in buildings.[11] They can walk through walls.[12] Christ's Spirit shows no racism, sexism, or favoritism.[13] It takes on whatever form it inhabits.[14] It can permeate the womb of the unborn.[15] God's Holy Spirit dwells within us (*Eight Verses that Show Jesus Christ Lives in You*).

I never realized just how much I trusted in myself and in my own abilities rather than God and His Spirit until I experienced a deep rejection within the church when I started to surrender to Him. I wanted to re-box Him up and hold onto those things I knew that were safe and comfortable and accepted for a time, but I kept feeling His deep beckoning to trust Him and His will for my life. I would be lying if it wasn't a constant tug of war at times, but I've learned that the only way I experience deep satisfaction comes when I surrender and trust Him and take the risks that He's calling me to. It lights my path and gives my life flavor.

SALT AND LIGHT

Desire of the nations
By Your flesh and blood You fed
Yet we feed only rations
Of our stale old bread

We eat just enough
Of our religiosity
That we've forgotten what it means
To be truly hungry

We try to stave off the desire
Of the forever starving
For their works are revealed through fire
Threatening our mediocrity

So afraid of heretical fakes
We dare not cross a line
Terrified of mistakes
Any risk we decline

So we tiptoe in shallow water
Forgetting You walked on the deep end
We'd lose our control if we went farther
And on You, we'd need to depend

Intimidated by darkness
We cover our eyes
We no longer love recklessly
To our own demise

We're called to be the light of the world, a city on a hill,
The salt of the earth

Now, we've lost our flavor
We've lost our worth

We've forgotten Living Water
Won't be contained in a box
And any attempt to put You in
Neglects to feed Your flock

We live in false luxury
Pushing away Your Comforter
Or choose false humility
Accusing many-a law breaker

We've forgotten our strength is our joy
And the gospel means good news
Our salvation never came by works
Yet that is the life we choose

We are to be known by our love
And love never fails
Yet we're known by our rights
And all that entails

Or we take another route
And encourage any sin
Meant to walk in spotless purity
Of the world we're in

We don't question anymore
Playing know-it-alls
The gods we've built live in
Any of our four walls

We need to tear down religious idols

Our minds we need You to refresh
We are the circumcision meant to worship in Spirit
Having no confidence in our flesh

We want to be salt to the earth
We long to be the light
Our playing small never served our world
Nor put up any fight

The safest place is in Your will
And that's where we long to be
Led by Your Spirit
However daunting

WHEN WE FREE ourselves and follow God's Spirit, He'll most likely lead us into wilderness seasons. He might give us dreams, visions, and prophecies He wants us to share without any regard to our gender[16] even if we go to a church that seeks to silence us. God will never do things the way we think He will and will always require our trust. However, I've found that when I try to see the journey as an adventure that He's calling me to and trust Him, I have found the peace and rest my soul deeply longs for and continually seeks.

Reflect:

IS THERE anything you feel like God is calling you to do that you or the people around you keep saying can't be from God? What is it, and why is that?

. . .

I would encourage you to pray that God speaks to you and through you. Pray that He gives you dreams and visions and understanding to follow His leading.

So often, we seek to limit God and our experiences and do what feels safe and comfortable instead of trusting Him. I often wonder if that's why we base our lives on those we read about in the Bible. We seek to formulate our life so much because we don't know how to surrender and trust.

Unless what you feel like God is leading you to do or say goes in direct contradiction to His Word, I would encourage you to pursue it. There is wisdom in seeking godly advice from others. I'm not suggesting you don't do that. However, "seek a second or third opinion" from people you know are intimate with God, and don't limit Him and others' experiences if you feel like someone is trying to hold you back in fear or because they haven't learned what it means to truly surrender. When we surrender to God knowing He has our best in mind and follow His lead, we can find rest for our souls.

13

REST

"Come to Me, all you who are weary and burdened, and I will give you rest. Take My yoke upon you and learn from Me, for I am gentle and humble in heart, and you will find rest for your souls. For My yoke is easy and My burden is light."
Matthew 11:28-30 (NIV)

This is what the Sovereign Lord, the Holy One of Israel, says: "In repentance and rest is your salvation, in quietness and trust is your strength, but you would have none of it."
Isaiah 30:15 (NIV)

"A woman who is at rest with herself has nothing to prove to others. She embraces her strengths and cheers others on with a pure heart. Her light shines brightly, her words are seasoned with kindness and grace. She is peaceful and edifies others as

she is secure in her Heavenly Father's love."
Hanna Bryant

"Oh, so you're a role wife," my life coach said as he explained that the reasons my husband had listed as to why I mattered to him were all based on the roles I fill in his life. I was encouraged to see a life coach and mentor from the women's pastor at our church after my most recent news of a third degree prolapse made me feel like I could no longer mentally hold myself together anymore. Unsurprisingly, the areas that I was physically torn apart in are the very areas that women hold a lot of tension in when they've had issues with the males in their lives. My husband's constant need for performance and image, his push for me to be like his mother in certain areas, and my overwhelming drive for excellence caused me to never feel like I could rest. However, it went deeper than that.

During this journey, I felt led to read *The Dance of the Dissident Daughter*. In it, Sue Monk Kidd describes "The Favored Daughter," which I found myself relating to. In it she says the following:

> One of the more uncomfortable discoveries I made about myself during this time was a need to prove myself to the father-world—my own father, the cultural father, the church father. The powerful male presence. I began to recognize how important it was to me that he be aware of my accomplishments. The need surfaced from a deep place in my feminine wound.
>
> I'd grown up the firstborn in a field of bright, athletic brothers, unconsciously trying to convince everyone that being a girl was every bit as worthy. Certainly no one ever said to me

that girlhood was less valuable. I simply picked it up by virtue of being female on the planet. And I set out to prove it wrong. I tried through a blaze of achievement: "A"s on the report card, school honors, swimming trophies, cheerleading trophies, church awards. I did it through compliance. I did it by being everything I imagined a good girl should be.

It had been a core pattern in my life, this attempt to be a Favored Daughter.

Favored Daughters are women who, carrying the wound of feminine inferiority, try to make up for it by seeking the blessing of the cultural father. Through accomplishments and perfectionism we hope to atone for the "original sin" of being born female. We are hoping that Father God will eventually see our worth.

Even as an adult woman, I'd set up perfectionist standards, which kept me striving. I pursued a thin body, happy children, an impressive speech, and a perfectly written article with determination to succeed, but also with an internal voice that led me to feel whatever I did wasn't quite enough. I worried about not measuring up.

Herein lies the torment of it: Favored Daughters strive for their worth, piling up external validations, but inside they are most often plagued by self-doubt, wondering if their worth or their efforts are good enough.

I realized my own parents' wounds and desire to work out their salvation were rubbing off on me—this constant need to prove myself. This came from my mother's drive for perfection, and what seemed like a fear of sin, mistakes, and messes within our home. It came from messages my parents heard about obedient children being a reflection of them. It came from my dad's views on femininity and women. There were also the incessant messages and Bible studies that highlighted the way to please God, my husband, and others was to be as the Proverbs 31 woman. When I got married, I took all that upon myself as I literally tried to fulfill all the roles and needs of everyone around me with excellence. Yet no matter how hard I strived, it never felt like enough. I didn't feel loved unless I was fulfilling all my roles well. I also didn't realize just how much I might be projecting those messages onto God.

During this time, a quote I loved and shared on social media years before popped up that I was now having a hard time digesting. I penned my thoughts in my journal that night.

> "Continually restate to yourself what the purpose of your life is. The destined end of man is not happiness, nor health, but holiness. Nowadays we have far too many affinities, we are dissipated with them; right, good, noble affinities which will yet have their fulfillment, but in the meantime, God has to atrophy them. The only thing that matters is whether a man will accept the God who will make him holy. At all costs, a man must be rightly related to God."
>
> — OSWALD CHAMBERS

God,

I shared this today on Facebook eight years ago. I had it in my old Precious Moment's Bible I loved long before then, written on one of my pages reserved for special quotes that I loved, yet today I read it and struggled with it.

Lately, I've shared verses with the kids talking about freedom and how, "where the Spirit of the Lord is, there is freedom . . . " and "it is for freedom that Christ has set us free, therefore do not be tangled again to a yoke of slavery..."

I wrote most of a whole chapter called "Free Your Spirit," and my parents just visited and left yesterday morning, which was good, but as always, I struggled with my mom and my dad's beliefs . . .

I hate the sense of duty, shame, and obligation I feel around them. It's almost like I feel repulsed or devoid of any energy to help at all after being around them when usually I want to help people. Usually, my want to be of help fuels me. My exhaustion still hasn't picked up since they came . . .

We watched Gilmore Girls tonight—Drew, Bella, and I. I had this strong longing to be fully known and loved, quirks and all, with no expectations from me—no obligations or roles to fulfill, just to be wholly loved and enjoyed for myself. Thinking about that thought makes me want to cry. There's a part of me I realized that ties religion—maybe even to You if I'm projecting—to duty, obligation, responsibility, and shame. It's the need to be perfect or always striving for perfection and holiness—this need to want to become the perfect woman and flawless (or the "Proverbs 31 woman" if you will) in order to please You—possibly in order to be loved.

I've always leaned in and tried to conquer challenges so they didn't deter me, and I've always had to prove myself all my life, but lately the thought of needing to prove myself or the thought of needing to conquer another challenge is wearing me out before I've even begun. Even worse, it's actually making me feel angry . . . so angry, and I don't know what to do with it. I feel like I'm going to explode.

Part of me feels like I'm on the verge of an "awakening" as Sue Monk Kidd shared in her book *The Dissident Daughter* I started to read. Part of me is terrified of where my anger might take me and how out of control I might feel if I let loose. Part of me is threatened by the thought that I'm being selfish and self-worship is the "national religion of hell." The other part of me is full of excitement for a new adventure where exploring these thoughts might take me, but I also feel tension in my whole body that is scaring the crap out of me.

I didn't really plan for any of this, and I feel like it's going to shift everything in my life and might not be readily accepted by others or myself. I've been with people where love has always felt so conditional to the roles I play—to fulfilling others' needs or wants, to making others happy, or meeting their expectations—and I've just been growing so weary never feeling like I'm enough, certainly never more than enough. I just don't know what exploring this will look like—if I'll be acting selfish or pegged for selfish and criticized and shamed if I don't meet others' expectations. I just feel stuck. Stress-paralyzed. I'm worried how staying where I am in this place might just be passed onto my daughters and their daughters and a thousand generations of women wishing for women brave enough to explore and conquer this and share their stories and change the world. I feel so small when I think of that possibility—so ill-equipped and unworthy. I feel like this journey is from You, these things and the thought process I need to conquer is from You to help me and others heal, but it feels so foreign to everything I've ever heard about women and what we're expected to do and be as Christian women. . .

Yet expectation kills relationships . . .

And I feel this deep suffering in my soul as I hear expectations and Christianity linked together and projected onto You.

If You hadn't healed my collarbone when I was four and my deep desire to know, love, kiss, and hug You as a result before I could possibly meet or even know Your expectations, I can't even imagine where I'd be or how much my relationship with You would have suffered if I only pegged You by the box You've been put in.

Is the purpose of life really to be holy or free?

"It is for freedom that Christ has set us free . . . "

Was freedom only given for us to be free to choose holiness? Does holiness mean perfection and without flaw? Is holiness expected of us? Feeling loved without expectation made me want to please You before I knew how, but I believe in that desire and response You were pleased—thrilled even. I want that again. Surely this has nothing to do with selfishness . . .

I love You. Deep down, I know I always have and always will. I wish I could please You with my life more than anything, and I wish I could feel Your closeness and love again.

Why does it feel like I'm struggling?

Taking down/coming against spiritual strongholds and generational curses . . . ?

Oh God, I need Your strength. Help me! God of mercy, come to my aid.

> Yours Always,
> -Rachel Ann

As I was reading about Jesus' baptism, I realized all over again what God said about Jesus: "This is My beloved Son, in whom I am well pleased."[1] It was before He even started His ministry. Jesus hadn't performed a single recorded miracle yet. He hadn't done any job worth noting in Scripture, yet God was pleased with Him and proud of His Sonship. I think that right there helped fuel Him for ministry. It prepared Him for the wilderness, knowing that His worth didn't lie in His ability to perform but rather in what God said about Him. It was the foundation He needed to build upon so that everything He did was as a response to God's love for Him, rather than a constant striving for His approval. It allowed Him to produce from a place of rest, trusting in a Love that wasn't conditional to His performance or placing insurmountable demands and expectations on Him. It was entirely free and unmerited—the very thing we need to know and experience if we want to rest in God's love and live a life of service in response to Him.

It helped me knowing that God healed my collarbone at age four, before I fully knew right from wrong or the devastating consequences that could come from disobedience. It was so incredibly beneficial that I was restored not as a result of someone's elaborate prayers or anything I could have done. It is so healing for me to acknowledge that God cared enough about me to hear my thoughts and respond to the desires of my little heart. Knowing and meditating on all those truths is enough for me to want to live a lifetime of service to Him, feeling entirely grateful, undeserving, and forever indebted to Him, overwhelmed by the thought that I am loved by the Maker of Heaven and earth. It allows me to serve and obey Him from a place of rest.

Yet when I confuse the messages I've received in life and project it onto Him feeling like I will never meet the expectations demanded from me, it zaps any energy and desire to even want to try to please Him or others. Even worse, then I know I'll be judged for not living up to others' expectations of me. I could work my heart out and still be found lacking or barely getting by. It's like going on a never-ending treadmill without a stop button trying to earn love and knowing that if you were to stop and take a break, you'd fail miserably and be unable to get back on. When we serve from a place of lack—trying to earn and perform for love, even if we are completely and entirely loved—you can bet that our enemy will try to twist it into the reason we're loved. Then, as any son or daughter would, we'll be constantly wanting to test His love for us. *"If I did this, would God still love me?"* Our hearts would desperately want to know. And if we were really to test that out, we would be met with feelings of shame and unworthiness, fearful of coming before a holy God's presence.

God so badly wants us to know His perfect love that casts

out all fear.[2] He wants us to know that it's by grace we have been saved through faith, not by works.[3] We can do nothing to earn His love, and there's nothing we can do to have it taken away.[4] While He desires obedience and love, He wants it to come as a response to His abundant love for us, not as a sacrifice, continually striving for His approval.[5] In repentance and rest is our salvation. In quietness and trust is our strength.[6] He wants us to "be still and know" who He is and that He is with[7] those who are made in His image.[8] Our worth comes from nothing we do and lies in the value He placed in us[9] and the high price He paid for us.[10] When we know this, we can serve from a place of rest.

Reflect:

I WANT to encourage you to get a piece of paper and write down the following: "This is my beloved daughter, (insert name), in whom I am well pleased." Now, place it next to the mirror you look in most. Every time you get ready for the day or just glance in the mirror, I'd encourage you to speak it out over yourself, meditating on God saying that to you. Keep saying it until you believe it deep down. You'll know when that is by the choking back of tears, the tears streaming down your cheeks, the smile on your face, or the extra pep in your step. If you want to, keep it there even after you "know it." We could all use the reminder.

Often, after we feel like we've failed the most, we need to hear it more. If our worth doesn't lie in what we do, it can't be taken away from us by what we fail to do or when we mess up. We'll explore those thoughts more in the next chapter.

14

KNOW YOUR WORTH

"Your value doesn't decrease based on someone's
inability to see your worth."
Ted Rubin

For You created my inmost being;
You knit me together in my mother's womb.
I praise You because I am fearfully and wonderfully made;
Your works are wonderful, I know that full well.
My frame was not hidden from You
when I was made in the secret place,
when I was woven together in the depths of the earth.
Your eyes saw my unformed body;
all the days ordained for me were written in Your book
before one of them came to be.
How precious to me are Your thoughts, God!
How vast is the sum of them!
Were I to count them,

>   they would outnumber the grains of sand—
>   when I awake, I am still with You.
>   Psalm 139:13-18 (NIV)

I was almost nineteen years old when I had my first kiss. It was the shortest relationship I had been in at that point—about five months in—but we had so many confirmations that it was meant to be. I was smitten. He was obsessed. Things seemed too good to be true. It wouldn't take much longer for me to find that indeed, they were.

When we were starting our relationship, I was completely honest about who I was and what I had done. I had physical reservations, but I didn't really carry any shame from my past. I was looking forward to the day I could finally "let loose" and feel free to express myself sexually within the boundaries of marriage. My reservations weren't due to being stuck up or prudish, but they had everything to do with protection of my heart and emotions and wanting to bless another from everything I had read and heard. I already had such a hard time cutting soul ties in the past and never wanted to bring that into my marriage—for mine and my future husband's sake. While I prayed for my future husband and his relationships, I honestly never expected the same in return.

My boyfriend, Drew, on the other hand, carried a lot of shame—only I didn't know it yet. In fact, he hid it so well, he made me think that he was on the same page as me physically. I was surprised when he said he didn't hug the opposite sex either and had such a clean slate. He told me constantly how hard it was to find a great Christian girl like me, and he made me feel like I was rare and amazing with his overwhelming pursuit.

Drew went right along with my boundaries initially. We

didn't hold hands or even hug at first, yet our relationship was moving very fast emotionally it seemed. With so many confirmations that it was meant to be, I welcomed it. I felt safe and loved and was enthusiastic that all my pent-up energy could finally be put into someone and something tangible. It was about a year into the wilderness season I was getting into that I had met him. His charm, good looks, and seemingly strong desire for me overpowered any hesitation I had about us. I thought I felt God's love through him more than anyone else and wrote about it not long after we met.

INSIDE OF YOU

My Lover hid His face from me
Hid in a corner to see
If I would run after Him
Then I must be
The beloved He came to chase

The night was long and hard
The sun beat down the days
I whispered for Him in my closet
I cried out for Him in the crowds
But He seldom showed His face

Oh Beloved, I need You
I can't go on for long
Give me a glimpse of Your beauty
Let me see Your face
Show me with You I belong

For the days seem so long now
The nights are so hard

My dreams have lost the hope
Of seeing a glimpse of Your beauty
And finding where You are

But just when I started to give up
I saw You in an unusual place
It wasn't where I looked before
It was a place I failed to see
For I found You in his face

Who are you, my beloved?
Who are you who has His face?
Who are you who pursues me,
Who never stops seeking me,
And shows me His amazing grace?

Who am I, so unworthy
To be loved by such a wonder as you?
You've opened up Heaven
Revealed my Lover
And I found Him inside of you

His family seemed to welcome me as well. In fact, so much so, that our first Christmas together I got more from these strangers than I had ever gotten from my own family. Not to mention, he bought me the best camera I had ever owned at the time. It was all so overwhelming.

It bewildered me when he bragged about getting practice making out with a past girlfriend who was at his parents' house in her bikini when we visited or when he whispered that a girl who liked him gave him a hug at a wedding. Drew had already told me he didn't hug girls, but then hugged her right in front of me. I was hurt when two steps into a song at that wedding, he told me I couldn't dance as he left to dance with his sister. I found it perplexing when Drew and some of his family members and several people at that same wedding we went to kept trying to get us to kiss when my family encouraged my standards. I tried to tell myself that it was just a different culture than I was used to and made excuses for it. I thought that maybe they just didn't take physical touch as seriously and maybe I took things too seriously. After all, I knew I was going to marry him.

While I didn't give into letting him kiss me any of those times in front of others, I gave him the ok the next day on the ten-hour trip back to my hometown. My first kiss was met with criticism and ended with him crying because he felt ashamed for pressuring me. I was so incredibly confused by all that had happened, how it got so physical so fast, the shame of giving in, and also the fear of being a bad kisser. I can't say that fear had never crossed my mind before, but I never imagined my first experience being responded to in that way. I had so many guys in my past trying to convince me to let down my guard with that same excuse that I might be bad at it, to which I'd reply that I had a lifetime of practicing with my husband, so I wasn't worried. Now, it felt like maybe I should've been.

The next time, I tried to reassure Drew that it was my choice and wanted to prove I could do a better job. I wasn't criticized the second time, but while I was so focused on my performance, I didn't realize just how far it would be taken. I remember looking at the ceiling wondering why God wasn't stopping this, frantically questioning how on earth we got to this point so soon and wondering if I had lost my virginity. We didn't have sex, but we went way farther than I was prepared for. He couldn't have possibly known how much shame I would carry from the experience or how worthless I felt when the one thing I thought set me apart and that all Christian guys wanted was taken from me. He couldn't have known how much baggage I'd carry from then on when I'd hear from other well-intentioned women that guys only go as far as a girl will let them as though guys are helpless creatures who can't uphold themselves to high standards on their own. As if it was a girl's fault when a guy took it too far. Drew was six years older than me, was far more "experienced," and merely thought it was something I'd enjoy. The very next day, he proposed. I tried to tell myself that at least we were going to get married, so maybe it was ok. At that moment, I felt like no other guy would want me then anyways after what had happened.

To say that I regretted how far we went would be an understatement, yet once things turned physical, it was hard to go back. We were technically virgins when we got married, but the heart behind our actions showed that was just a technicality. I had written a poem not long after drawing on others' thoughts and my own experience trying to help others not get into the same situation that we found ourselves in.

WHAT'S BEEN DONE AND WHAT'S TO COME

It's the pieces of you
The ones you can never get back
But you want to
It's the heart you gave away
That still beats where it's at
Away from you

It's the first kiss
You always miss
You would get back if you could
It's the time you lost
Punishment's cost
If you could take back you would

It's seeing others repeat
The same mistakes you made
In a heartbeat
Wanting to "live life"
Give it a chance
With their own two feet

Running the same course
You tried to hide
To protect others from taking
It's the void you could never lose
With meaningless nothings
In the remaking

Humble yourself now
Understand we've made mistakes
We want something better for you
Our road, do not retake
We can't get back what we've lost
And brothers and sisters,
We don't want you to lose it
Satan doesn't want you to see sin's cost
But he'll show you
The moment you abuse it

God has prepared
Something better for you and me
A life with no regrets
For all eternity
So don't give in
To pleasure for a season
A lifetime of pleasure
Is more than we can reason

> But if you've already lost it
> Don't give up, don't give in
> Satan wants you to think it's over
> When God wants you to be forgiven
> Move on now
> What's done is done
> You can't change the past
> But you can foretell what's to come

THREE OR FOUR MONTHS LATER, the shame Drew was carrying got to be too much as he vented all he had done in the past over the phone while I was at work. It was a lot to take in, but I accepted him with "open arms." Although I was angry about the lies that he'd believed that ever made him feel unworthy of me over something that was meant to be a blessing and breathed a huge sigh of relief that at least we were going somewhere, I wished I had known about his experience from the beginning. All this newfound information had me feeling like I was going to be marrying a stranger. I realized how much we still needed to get to know one another, especially with me moving three hours away from anyone else I knew to be with him. I started wondering what I was getting into.

Drew seemed to think I was encroaching on his freedom and expecting perfection from him when I asked for honesty. From then on, other girls would be met with flattery and charm, while I'd be criticized over every little thing or told how ridiculous I was for not being ok with it. As our relationship continued, I began to realize things weren't as they seemed and lost any trust I had once possessed. A wall started forming around my heart, and I felt so incredibly unsafe and lost, unable to be won.

"WON" LOST GIRL

Walls closing in, so silently
So slowly
And yet, so suddenly
I just never took the time to notice
Because I thought you noticed me
And I need not have to worry
How wrong I have been
Slowly slipping in
To everything
I've always wanted to run away from
What have I become?
A shadow of one I love
Who notices not the lack thereof?
Of passion, of romance, of love
And yet, I notice
Is this all there is?
Is this what I've held out for?
To have my dreams shattered,
To have my screams ignored?
To take care of myself-
Because nobody else cares anymore
I just want to run
I'm so scared and I just want to run
Run away from all of this
In hope of a future ending in bliss
And I know no one's perfect
And I know you mean well
But I feel like I'm in freaking hell
And you don't care that I'm burning
You don't even notice
And I wish you would stop saying that you're learning
To pursue me

And just pursue me for once
Before I run away
And you're too proud
To admit and chase
The lost girl you "won"

I wish I could say that I knew my worth, set boundaries, or kicked him out when he treated me so badly because I would never have permitted my daughters to be treated in the same way. However, I didn't. In fact, I felt so worthless, that the more I found out, the more I felt intimidated by other girls rather than being able to celebrate their beauty. Other women started feeling more like my competition the more insecure I felt. I didn't know what was happening to me as I had never really dealt with that in my past. It was much harder knowing I was "supposed" to marry Drew, and every time I wanted to leave, he'd say just the right thing or use gifts to get me to stay, telling me how much better it'd be once we got married.

I knew it was a lie. I told him marriage doesn't magically solve anything and was worried about the impending bitterness that I felt growing inside of me as I wondered if there wasn't a way to make it stop. Still, I stayed. I had already dropped out of college, moved back home, and was working to pay off school loans and pitch in for our wedding. I was so afraid of disappointing others that I didn't know how to stand up for myself. Not to mention the fact that he was the only guy I had ever really been physical with. We always heard how perfect we looked together, and I reminded myself of all the confirmations we had, but so much of it felt like obligation at that point. I didn't feel safe or loved in the least, but I never felt at peace about ending it either. While we looked the part, there was a lot missing in our unhealthy relationship.

WHAT'S MISSING

Obligation leaves our spirit left for dead
Deadening the drive for words left unsaid
And where did we go wrong?
What happened to the passion that belongs?
Hearts once opened, now closed
Once love natural
Now we pose
To fit a picture perfect expectation
Of how we're supposed to be
We look so lovely
In my painted face
And our natural grace
But underneath
Not a trace
Of what's needed
I feel so defeated
And we look so perfect
How could I leave?
And I love you
But do you love me?
I remind myself of old memories
Of how you swept me off my feet
But now you've opened your arms
And I wish I was unharmed
I wish my feet would hit the floor
I wish there was something more
That something missing
That we had in the beginning
I wish you were you
And I was me

> And God still gave you grace
> To find me captivating enough
> To want me

IN CASE YOU'RE WONDERING, marriage didn't solve our problems. It only made them so much worse as marriage often does. It was all so messed up. Rather than release and let go or follow through with my gut, I clung tighter—at times desperate for Drew's approval. I felt like used up goods that no longer held value. I didn't speak up against false accusations or beliefs about me. I always expected him to set the record straight, but those expectations were never met.

I carried with me so much shame, baggage, hurt, unforgiveness, and bitterness for years. What I mentioned was just the tip of the iceberg. I allowed so much of what I carried to shape me into a person I hated—a person I was no longer proud to be. My view of my worth was overshadowed by everything I had done wrong. It was clouded by mistakes and regrets, what ifs, and what I should have done differently. It was molded by others' thoughts and opinions of me—despite many of them being untrue.

Even worse, those things that I once called out and thought were so beautiful in other women and friends were seen as competition and no longer met with celebration. It was so incredibly hard to hear about some of those traits I once possessed that seemed to be thrown in my face. I often found myself cutting other women down, saying that they would become insecure or unattractive if they were put through the same things. I felt like such a victim, yet at the same time, blamed myself for being in such a bad relationship. I allowed it to go too far, and I seemed incapable of setting boundaries and speaking up for myself. Inside, I felt so incredibly ugly taking out my frustrations secretly over other women I would have acknowledged and honored in the past. Looking back, I realize I allowed myself to be treated so badly because I didn't think highly of myself or think I deserved any better. As Stephen Chbosky states in *The Perks of Being a Wallflower*, "We accept the love we think we deserve."

Some days, I wish I could go back to my former self and tell her what I know now. Our worth cannot be taken away or stolen from us. It's not something we can give away and not get back. It's something we possess deep within and reflect. It is not even determined by the value we place upon ourselves as we can be deceived and sell ourselves short.

However, it has everything to do with what our Creator says about us. It lies in the way we are fearfully and wonderfully crafted in the image of God, knit together by the Almighty in our mother's womb.[1] It has to do with the plans God has for us,[2] the work promised to be completed in us,[3] and the high price Jesus paid for us on the cross.[4] Our worth is not determined by a broken soul that doesn't know our worth, let alone theirs. It's time we stop listening to the broken people in our lives and the fractured relationships we get ourselves into to try to make us whole, tell us who we are, and determine our worth. It's time we reclaim ourselves and become everything God has created us to be.

Reflect:

HOW HAS PURITY CULTURE, promiscuity, and relationships affected the way you view yourself and your worth?

. . .

I SHARED about how purity culture was damaging to my and my husband's relationship. In what ways can we improve the ways we talk about purity and sexuality?

Do you find yourself trying to find your worth or wholeness in a relationship? What would happen if that relationship were to end? Do you think you would be any less valuable or whole without a relationship? If so, why?

WHAT DOES God say about your worth?

IN THE NEXT CHAPTER, I will be sharing how to reclaim a part of your identity that will never change.

15

RECLAIM

"For as long as you can remember, you have been a pleaser, depending on others to give you an identity. You need not look at that only in a negative way. You wanted to give your heart to others, and you did so quickly and easily. But now you are being asked to let go of all these self-made props and trust that God is enough for you. You must stop being a pleaser and reclaim your identity as a free self."
Henri Nouwen

"Women have essentially become the products of the societies and traditions into which they were born and bred. As a woman, you might not like who you are, yet your self-concept probably came from the environment in which you were raised. If the nations of the world had understood God's purposes for women and men, they would have realized that the spirit of equal rights that demands equality from men was never intended by God, because He has already made men and women equal. Men and women were created equal. Men and women are equal. That's not for a senate or a congress to decide. God already made this decision in creation. Again, when you allow others to declare who you are, you are submitting your rights to them, and you must be prepared for the consequences. Don't ever give anybody the right to say what kind of human value you have. Don't let anybody else tell you how much of a person you are. When you understand that equality is inherent and discover how it is to be manifested in your life, then you can begin to live in the full realm of that equality, regardless of what others tell you about yourself."

Dr. Myles Munroe

"I will be a Father to you, and you will be my sons and daughters, says the Lord Almighty."
2 Corinthians 6:18 (NIV)

I looked into the mirror and cried as flashbacks came back to me. My newborn was only four days old, and all I wanted to do was rest and enjoy her, but the severe sleep deprivation and image staring back at me in the mirror were sending PTSD-like flashbacks that were playing games with my mind. The last time I felt like this was after the birth of my second child who came a year after my first, and I found out my body had gone into survival mode.

"Do you see your husband as your teacher?" our pastor asked as we sat down to discuss our marital issues. I laughed incredulously, knowing why we were there, only to see he wasn't joking. In that moment, with my response, it seemed perfectly clear to our pastor why we were struggling the way we were. In his mind, my lack of submission to Drew as my teacher caused him to continually betray me.

It didn't matter that I was the only one seeking God in our marriage or trying to make it work. It didn't matter that in all my years of emotional neglect and oppression, I had never experienced those as much as I had during my marriage. My expectations for him at the time were about as low as they could get. My only requirements were honesty and faithfulness, yet even those weren't being met. There was no trust, no pursuit, no love, no touch even—unless he wanted something in return. He no longer seemed to be attracted to me or my body, and he felt no shame in telling me so.

Sleep was another issue in our marriage. My sleep was never seen as a necessity, my preferences never a consideration—only his. When our second child was born so quickly after our first with a completely opposite schedule to our one-year-old, I was sent to another room so my husband could get sleep. After being told by the doctor my lack of sleep was detrimental to my health and it was of utmost importance, I got my husband to help at night. Even still, I often cried myself to sleep as my husband spouted off his frustrations.

It wasn't long after that when I saw what was on our computer. When confronted, my husband constantly denied or blame-shifted in a way that made me feel like I was going crazy. Nothing ever got resolved. This time, we had recently finished our first marriage class where he had affirmed to the class that I still treated him like we were dating. It dawned on me that no one deserved to be treated the way he was treating me—not even me, who was always trying so hard to please. When I said I didn't know if I could keep staying in a relationship with someone who could continually lie even when I knew the truth beyond a shadow of a doubt, it was my lack of encouragement that was the problem he professed.

I was over carrying the weight of the false accusations and misplaced blame in our relationship. I was over being told I was so lucky to be with a good-looking guy who did more than the dads in our lives just because he worked up his charm and people pleasing in front of others. I had no idea how to set up boundaries at that point. The little sleep I got was filled with nightmares of being stuck in a web with giant spiders above my head coming down towards me. Those were the first and only times I ever remember waking up frantically screaming or gasping for air. I felt so incredibly trapped and stuck in my waking life.

TEARS OF ANGUISH streamed down as I buried my face into my hands and fell to the ground of our bathroom. It was the middle of the night, and I was wondering how in the world I let myself get back in this place. Mentally, I felt stuck. Only this time, I didn't even have to be asleep to relive my nightmares. I didn't feel like I could escape this internal prison, the rejection of my own body, and the inner battle I thought I had already fought and won. As much as my husband and our lives looked so different and better than they had back then, here I was reliving those moments as though they hadn't passed. I just sat and cried out to God that night in fear that I would be stuck in this place, but then I felt God's tender presence come over me and give me hope. Although I felt so alone when I went through this the first time, I knew God would be there with me this time leading me through every step of the way, teaching me how to heal from the inside out.

One morning I came across a Bible verse I'd read plenty of times before, saying how we're the apple of God's eye. I read it in the Passion Translation and the sub note listed at the bottom made my eyes well up with tears. It said, "Protect me from harm; keep an eye on me like you would a *daughter* reflected in the twinkling of your eye. Yes, hide me within the shelter of your embrace, under your outstretched arms."[1]

I recalled when Drew and I first hung out with our pastors after moving to a new state. My sweet women's pastor basically told me that I could assess whether the treatment in my marriage was acceptable or not based on if I would permit my daughters to be treated the way I was. Would I idly sit back and watch it happen, or would I feel led to speak up and say something? If I would speak up for them, what was stopping me from speaking up for myself? As I snapped back to reality, I started questioning when I lost my voice. When did I just sit back and become a victim in my life, passively accepting whatever came my way or whatever anyone spoke over me as though I didn't have a say?

Even more, I felt like God was asking me when I stopped being a daughter. That no matter what age I am, no matter what role I play as a wife and mom, I am still first and foremost a daughter to Him—a daughter of the King of Kings. While I haven't always felt the shelter of His embrace or His outstretched arms keeping me from harm, He's always been there loving me with a twinkling in His eye.

Despite the disgust I felt towards myself and my reflection, I had this overwhelming urge come upon me to look deeply into the mirror and encourage myself as I would another person in my position or even my own daughters if they were struggling. I spoke God's truth over myself and my body. It beckoned me to take into account the miracle of life my body just produced and the hatred and jealousy our enemy has for all life that is created in the image of God. It shed light on the fact that if he could get me to believe that my worth lies solely on an outer shell that constantly changes, what society says is beautiful, or even another person, my value will always be in question. This body, this resilient temple that houses the Spirit of God, the spirit of me, that held six other humans and birthed and fed five, has gained and lost hundreds of pounds, and is still standing strong and surviving despite so many hard hits is a warrior that should be respected—a fearsome sight to behold. Those thoughts felt so foreign and hard to accept. Although I still struggle to accept them, I don't immediately reject them anymore.

It wasn't until my own experience with receiving marriage "help" that I truly realized just how great the injustice lay within the church. There was a part of me that always seemed to think that if we had marriage problems, and I just did X, Y, and Z, then I would get the desired result. However, the assumption that I was somehow failing in some way or that it was my fault when I checked all the boxes I could possibly check and then some, seemed unfair. The lack of responsibility brought upon my husband when he had a leadership role made me realize just how unhealthy the ideas being perpetuated were and how codependent I had allowed myself to become as a result of following the Christian teachings I had been taught.

I started asking myself what my purpose in life was? As a child, obeying my parents seemed to be the goal. As a woman, I'd been told that I was created to be *his*—my husband's—helpmeet. I felt called to be a mom. I only felt accepted and loved when I was meeting others' needs, making others happy, and living out roles that fulfilled others.

However, I started asking myself if I would still hold value if I never became a wife or a mom. What if I remained only a daughter? What about those who don't get married, are called to celibacy, or those who can't have kids? Do they still hold value within the church?

Years ago, I remember thinking it strange to learn that man was said to be both male and female before God ever formed Eve from man's side. I remember coming to the realization that

Adam gave Eve her name meaning "mother of all living"[2] before she ever even had any kids. While he was most likely speaking life over her, "washing her in the word" so to speak and prophesying over her future, I remember thinking how women must be life-givers whether they have kids or not. We are "womb-men" as Dr. Myles Munroe points out. It seemed the Bible reiterated that fact by saying the barren woman should rejoice in the fact that she has more children than that of the married woman.[3]

However, when I got married, it was as though I forfeited my voice for Drew's, yet God says in the last days, the sons and daughters will prophesy.[4] I started asking myself at what point did I stop playing my role as a daughter? How on earth could I tell my daughters that they only have worth when they are obeying commands, helping meet their husband's needs, or being a mom? How could I tell them they need to silence their voice within the church? How come I never heard the verses of Miriam being a prophetess[5] that could only have been appointed by God in the Old Testament and a leader of Israel[6] or any of the other female leaders in the Bible from the pulpit? Surely, we have worth apart from the roles we take on simply because we are God's daughters. Certainly, if God gave us a voice, we're meant to use it. If God's image is represented within males and females and the church extends beyond four walls and is the physical representation of Christ's body, we as women have a part in it. If there's no male or female in Christ, and we're supposed to submit to each other, there are no limits to what women can and can't do.

For so long, I let the voices of broken people have the influence over how I saw myself. I let them dictate my worth and tell me who I was as a woman. It was as though I was asking their permission, awaiting their approval, before I could come to accept myself. I often looked to the authority figures in my life, or even just the Christian men, to tell me who I was. Yet the overwhelming message I kept hearing was that God wanted women silent—seen and not heard—submissive servants to their husbands and joyful, sweet teachers to their children. A gentle and quiet spirit was to be sought after. As a loud, headstrong daughter who desired to please God more than anything, I felt I would never measure up. I was always too much or not enough. I felt ashamed for the way I was. I often felt like a foreigner in my own body, thinking there was a disconnect between my mind, body, and spirit.

As Dr. Myles Munroe explained in his book *Understanding the Purpose and Power of Woman*:

> . . . If you have to ask somebody for something, you are admitting that they have it; if you have to demand something from someone, you are confessing that they own it. When you do that, you are devaluing yourself, because you are, in effect, relinquishing the possession of your rights to someone else." He goes on to say, ". . . I am in control of whose opinions are important. There is a significant difference between demanding one's rights from someone and displaying the rights one already possesses. Do you really want to go to men and say, 'I demand equality with you,' implying that they have the power to make you equal? That is a dangerous thing to say. If you convince me that I have the power and the right to make you a whole person, then you are in trouble, because I could use it to play games with you, to manipulate you. I could use it to get what I want. I could give you some freedoms as I pleased—just enough to keep you in check—and withhold the rest. I believe that many people in movements for equality are inadvertently confessing that they have given over their rights to someone else.

As God led me on a path of healing, I felt the need to reclaim every part of my being and speak life over it. I needed to allow God to name me and tell me who I was in Him—not anybody else—and I needed to repent of all the times I allowed others' voices to have a greater say than God's. Those lies only held power because I believed them and continually re-played them in my mind. I didn't feel led to put down Drew, my dad, or any other person who might have failed to treat me as a whole being. My journey wasn't against men. It really wasn't about them either. This was about me.

If I didn't believe I was valuable apart from man, I would go on seeking his approval before I could accept myself. I would be walking around with a void in my life—susceptible to betrayal, seeking to fill a hole only God was meant to fill. I needed to believe that I was everything God wanted me to be and that who I was now and who He made me to be was just right for whatever path He led me on and anything He called me to. My mind, my body, my spirit, my voice are His creations, His masterpieces, and who am I to say they aren't enough and can't be used? Who am I to say I'm not enough exactly the way He made me? If I don't know my own value, how can I expect anyone else to know it either? I have to know that in Christ I am a whole being, not lacking any good thing, apart from anyone else— husband or kids—before I can ever wholly give of myself. I need to continually reclaim who I am and believe that everything I am is enough.

ENOUGH

You're not too much
Not too little
You don't just meet
Somewhere in the middle

You're not too tall
Not too short
You're not too anything
Of the sort

You're not too long
Not too wide
You don't have to shrink
Or move aside

You're not too loud
Not too quiet
Given a voice
Not kept private

You're not too shy
Not too bold
Not too young
Or too old

You're not too brown
Not too white
Not too pasty
You're just right

You're not gonna ruin
What God has for you

Not gonna miss
What He's called you to do

When you face your giants
You won't have to bluff
You'll find with God
You are just enough

Reflect:

AS A CHILD OF GOD, do you know that means you're royalty—a princess to the King of Kings? How would knowing that change how you view and conduct yourself, allow others to treat you, or influence how you treat others?

IF YOU SAW your son or daughter—or even another person for those who don't have kids—in a passive and painful position where he or she is constantly reacting and taking on the role of a victim, would you feel led to speak up?

Do you ever find yourself in that role? If so, what is stopping you from speaking up, taking charge, and reclaiming who you are?

EPHESIANS 2:10 SAYS, "For we are God's handiwork, created in Christ Jesus to do good works, which God prepared in advance for us to do." Do you believe you're God's handiwork, His creation, His masterpiece? Did you know that when God looked upon His creation, He saw that it was very good?[7] Do you believe that about yourself? If you did, what would change?

AFTER JESUS REAFFIRMED who He was and what He would tolerate when He was tempted by Satan for forty days and nights, Satan fled. Then, angels came and took care of Jesus.[8] Similarly, after a time of testing, we too must be refreshed and attended to. I'll share with you how I learned to take care of myself in the next chapter and hopefully give ideas on how you can too.

TAKE CARE

"Take care of your body. It's the only place you have to live."
Jim Rohn

"Do you not know that you are God's temple and that God's Spirit dwells in you? If anyone destroys God's temple, God will destroy him. For God's temple is holy, and you are that temple."
1 Corinthians 3:16-17 (ESV)

"Rest and self-care are so important. When you take time to replenish your spirit, it allows you to serve others from the overflow. You cannot serve from an empty vessel."
Eleanor Brown

I don't know when it started—feeling like I had to always take care of others and their needs before I took care of my own. Although I can't pinpoint when it started, I know I picked up the subtle messages all throughout my childhood. Many were well-intentioned and even helpful at getting me to consider others, but they often left me with an orphan mentality when it came to myself. With each growing need presented by our ever-growing family, I'd often mentally remind myself that I could sleep when I'm dead. Looking back, it's really no wonder that the slightest twist and subtlety of that half-truth could make me see death as an escape during extremely trying times. Pregnancies, though greatly wanted, often left me in a constant state of nesting, severe insomnia, and mental unrest as I tried to get things done or sneak a little time to myself into the quiet hours of the morning. It didn't help that I was already battling autoimmune disorders that tended to get worse with each pregnancy or that I had already suffered from a prolapsed uterus from my second-to-last pregnancy.

When I got pregnant with my last child, I began to suffer from severe depression. Drew had taken on more work at a different job, and we were in a better position financially than we'd ever been. We bought our first rental house that we flipped during the beginning of my pregnancy. Drew was a leader at church. We were living in a great house and had four beautiful kids that I was homeschooling. Everything in my life looked great from the outside. Yet, I kept envisioning myself in this beautiful dress in the middle of the ocean. My kids and all the demands I was carrying were like ropes that were pulling me down, and I was drowning. Nobody could see the tears forming in my eyes as the waves were washing them away. Yet, there was Jesus, standing on the water above me, so bright in contrast to the darkness I was in. He was reaching out His hand for me, and I so desperately wanted to grab it. I looked back at those precious children and the husband He had given me, knowing they were depending on me. They weren't burdens, yet this picture might make it seem that way, and I was too terrified to paint it.

I stumbled upon a quote by Tyler Knott Gregson one day after delivering my baby and wept. It said, "Promise me you will not spend so much time treading water and trying to keep your head above the waves that you forget, truly forget, how much you have always loved to swim."

Those things pulling me under were my dreams, my blessings, everything worth having in life. They were everything I loved and wanted for as long as I could remember. I knew God had made me fit for the job, yet the way I was carrying them was weighing me down and suffocating me.

I had always felt like the best things in life were worth working hard for and had never been intimidated by that, so I knew something was wrong. I knew right then and there that something had to change in my life. I couldn't wait around in the hopes that someone else would fill my tank. I couldn't keep hoping for someone else to rescue me. I couldn't keep pouring out from an empty tank. I couldn't keep trying to rescue others without putting on my oxygen mask first. I always hated the ideas of being a damsel in distress, yet I had become one.

My passivity and lack of ownership over my life and well-being were causing me to rely on others to meet my needs and fulfill my happiness, yet I was consistently found lacking. It was too much weight for another person to carry. Even worse, while I was so great at pinpointing everyone else's needs and wants—constantly writing down their likes and dislikes—I found myself unable to even name mine. I had no idea how I expected someone else to know what my needs were when I didn't know them myself. I had gone for so long without getting any needs or wants met that I started shutting down mentally and emotionally, seeking self-sufficiency.

If there was a need our family had, it went on my Christmas wish list. I'd always lived off of hand-me-downs and second-hand things and saw it as an opportunity to grow my creativity. However, it became a problem when I allowed my needs to continually become secondhand or worse. Everyone else in my care was suffering as a result of my irresponsibility to take care of myself.

I realized I didn't want to come to a point where I told my husband or kids that those days before them were the good old days as though I peaked in high school. I didn't want to keep telling them to live up to their potential and take care of themselves without modeling it and setting that example. I wanted to be able to honestly tell them the best is yet to come and live my life like it. God pressed upon my heart that the greatest gift I could give myself and those around me was to be the best version of myself I could be. Nobody else could make that decision for me. I had to make the choice and learn what it was that I needed to function at my best so I could better serve those in my care.

There was nothing selfish about it. If anything, I started noticing how often Jesus modeled it when He went off by Himself to find a quiet place and pray. It was His custom to go to the synagogue weekly on the sabbath day.[1] He had physical needs that needed to be met.[2] He had a "tribe."[3] He wept.[4] If anyone had the power to be self-sufficient, it was Jesus. Yet, He depended on God and His Word for His very breath[5] and did nothing by Himself.[6] I realized in trying to diminish myself and my needs, I was actually making my needs become greater than those around me by not properly attending to them in due time. They were consistently piling up and taking up valuable real-estate in my mind. I constantly fought resentment from meeting others' needs while I failed to attend to my own.

I had all the resources in front of me. I had a Husband in my Maker[7] who was more than willing to fill my love tank every single day. I had access to Living Water. I had a teacher in the Holy Spirit[8] who led me to those things outside of my immediate availability. I started taking classes with a *Living Free* program offered at church that I could attend for only the cost of a book and even got that marked off when I started helping co-facilitate them as their ministry matched my heartbeat. I started taking inexpensive but fun weekly dates with each of my kids that helped meet a need of mine and theirs. I joined a boot camp while our house was under construction so I could meet some physical needs, get some alone time, and work out in an atmosphere with others who had a similar goal. I woke up early enough to have a quiet time before working out and went early enough I could get home and shower before my husband woke up for work and without any kids banging on the door.

When the class closed down for a time due to the pandemic, I took part of my workout outside and took whichever older kids wanted to join to walk and jog a couple miles to a nearby park. When I struggled in different relationships, I followed the advice of a pastor friend and sought a life coach I met with several times who helped in that area. I bought my first vacuum and pair of new tennis shoes with money that I hadn't saved up from birthday or Christmas presents simply because there was a need, and we had the money. I started creating, writing, and blogging again, reading the Bible and other books, listening to podcasts, and finding resources to help grow myself in areas I wanted to learn in.

I began to set boundaries and speak up in areas I needed to. I told Drew I wanted to be able to look nice and get ready for church and needed his help with the kids on Sunday mornings. When he asked one day what area I could most use help in, I told him I'd love it if he helped with laundry as it was always a constant struggle to keep on top of it and I often found it the most overwhelming. He began to do it most of the time and watched all the sports he wanted while doing so and got my full support when the kids complained.

As the kids have gotten older, they've learned to help with their own laundry. Each of them has a designated room to keep clean each week as they grow and become more responsible. My hope is that their spouses won't carry the weight of their expectations, and if my kids have a spouse that picks up for them, they'll be extra appreciative. We stopped saying this is solely a man or woman's job and have learned to both pick up in areas that are needed at the time.

When Drew would be sitting in his La-Z Boy for hours on end while I was busy working to catch a break, I stopped being resentful and gave him options to do the dishes or put the kids to bed so we could both end the day together and relax. I stopped trying to control every area of my life and make everything perfect, and I started delegating in areas that I could.

I realized if I didn't want the generational weight and expectations placed upon women and the resentment that comes from it to continue for future generations, I'd need to model that instead of succumbing to the pressure to conform to the preconceived notions placed upon mothers. I began to show my daughters that they shouldn't carry the weight of the family alone and my sons that I respect them enough to expect more from them instead of treating them like they're helpless, lazy, and incapable. I show my husband that same respect and make sure to show my appreciation for it. I invest in the care of my health—physically, mentally, and spiritually—simply because there are needs that should be taken care of, and rest is one of them.

We all have different needs and wants, but I hope by sharing some of mine it will give you some ideas for your own life. If this is all new and you're used to doing everything on your own, some backlash is normal. There are growing pains for everyone getting out of his or her comfort zones, but I encourage you to stick with it and have a positive attitude as you share what you're going to do and what needs to be done in order to produce a peaceful environment.

Doing the same thing time and again and expecting different results is foolishness. Your spouse was attracted to you before you picked up after him. Show him that there's still more to you and more of you when you're not buried under the constant weight of meeting everyone else's needs but your own.

When the kids are too young to help, remember this is a season that will pass. It's so much easier to plant and cultivate seeds of helpfulness from the ground up than having to reboot and rebuild later on, though I know from experience that it is possible. When they are older, remind your children that "many hands make light work." If they live in your home, they can help keep it nice and create an atmosphere that's more enjoyable for everyone.

When you do everything as a mom, that experience will be all your family will ever know and expect from that position. As a result, you will constantly feel the pressure that comes from trying to meet those expectations, the resentment that comes when it is expected and unappreciated, and the feelings of failure that come when you don't meet those expectations. When you choose to be a woman who flows from a place of rest, you learn to find your worth apart from what you do. You will be doing yourself, your husband, and future generations a favor when you refuse to bow down as a servant and instead, rise up as a queen. In Proverbs 8:15, it says of the woman of wisdom that "by me, kings reign." Kings reign by queens, not servants.

A friend of mine told me there's a difference between caring for someone and taking care of someone. Even children know that it's not supposed to last forever, seeking independence as they grow. Failing to take care of myself caused me to develop a harmful codependency on my husband and kept my talents buried and my God-given dreams dormant.

Becoming healthier gives me the energy to invest in the talents God has given me and cultivate the seeds He's planted inside of me. As I've learned to step back, my husband has learned to rise to the plate and has become a more responsible, respectable, capable, and growth-minded man. He's started working out with me and reading on a regular basis, and he's stepped up in his fatherly role and as a husband. I'm honored to be married to him. As I learned to stand up and take care of myself rather than lean on and depend upon my husband, Drew grew more attracted to me as well. This journey has helped me to pinpoint my roles as a woman and better establish where I was meant to begin and end.

PIECED TOGETHER

I'm a river, I'm a stream
I can be the in-between
But I'm not Living Water
I get thirsty

I'm a mom
I'm a wife
But I'm not the Bread of Life
I get hungry

I can help meet a need
I can fertilize a seed
But I can't fill your void
I'm made to receive

I can make you less alone
I'm also flesh and bone
But I'm not the Holy Spirit

I get breathless

I can share in His glory
I can meet you in your story
But I don't begin or end
Like the Great I Am

I can care for you
I can add to what you do
But I can't make you whole
For I have gaps too

I can be your bride
'Til the day I die
But I'm not your caretaker
I'm to serve alongside

United, I want to build, grow, and abide
But if two wholes are not supplied
Our dreams will only collide
And we will divide what He wants to multiply

We're both but a piece
In the story of His plan
But, oh, what we could be
When we're pieced together

As I reclaimed my worth and learned to better take care of myself, I started re-envisioning what I wanted my life to look like. I knew that if I wanted growth in my life, I needed to be careful what I allowed into it.

Reflect:

WHAT ARE your basic human needs? Spiritual? Emotional?

WHAT NEEDS of yours are not being met?

WHAT CAN you do about it?

Do you find yourself depending on others to know and meet your needs without you knowing them yourself?

TAKE it a step further and think of ways you can function and live as your best self. What are areas you can improve on to help you reach your potential?

WHAT ARE unhealthy mindsets you can change?

Do you find it selfish to take care of yourself? If so, why?

CAN you see how not taking responsibility for the care of yourself can become a problem or how it in turn can become selfish in the long run?

17

SOW

"Those who sow with tears will reap with songs of joy."
Psalm 126:5 (NIV)

"The hard work of sowing seed in what looks like perfectly empty earth has a time of harvest. All suffering, pain, emptiness, disappointment is seed: sow it in God and He will, finally, bring a crop of joy from it."
Eugene H. Peterson

"For indeed I *am* for you, and I will turn to you, and you shall be tilled and sown."
Ezekiel 36:9 (NKJV)

I used to think of the principle of sowing and reaping sort of like karma—if you do something good, it will be returned to you. Likewise, for if you do something bad. The thing is, if something bad was going on in a person's life, then one could assume he or she probably deserved it. Job's friends thought the same. God ends up rebuking them for that.[1] Moreover, we don't see that really anywhere in the Bible. In the life of Job, Jesus, Joseph, Mary, Daniel, David—I could probably go on and on—God's favor seemed to put innocent lives in harm's way. When God showed His never-ending goodness and love in my own life, I experienced the same.

I wish I was as wise as Mary when God spoke things that seemed too good to be true in my life. Mary knew to bury the seeds of truth spoken to her deep inside her heart before they came to fruition.[2] In truth, I didn't fully understand what God had laid on my heart at the time. Like Joseph, God gave me big dreams that baffled me. Just like Joseph, I shared my dreams openly—or at least had them up for an hour on my blog before I was asked to take them down by my pastor. Snapped back to partial reality, I completely understood why I was asked to do so and did it willingly. It wasn't until four months after the event that my husband realized my feelings of rejection at church weren't unfounded when he was asked to be met with alone and questioned why I said what I did on social media. Apparently, my post was printed and shared around. I probably seemed like a mad woman to them. For almost three decades, I had happily served in the church in multiple areas. There were seasons I willingly and joyfully went several times a week. Decades I volunteered my time, skills, and money, and cheerfully loved and served the kids there. Yet, one mishap that lasted about an hour, and one would have thought I was an outcast.

I didn't quite understand the concept that favor with God

meant foolishness to man. I definitely never thought that some of the people I would experience the most rejection from in life were from those found in the church. I didn't realize just how much I cared about others' opinions until I felt the rejection from those that I thought were family. What felt like the best thing that could have possibly happened in my life at the time—God speaking to me again and showing He never stopped loving me at a time I felt too far gone to receive it—became something I was terrified of having repeated. It was the loss of control and a heightened awareness that the spiritual was even more present than I realized. I was afraid of ever being alone for a while after that. The experience of being so misunderstood and rejected after had me wanting to drown out the silence with noise if I was ever left to myself for fear that it might happen again.

It wasn't until later that I truly realized what Jesus was sharing in a parable found in Matthew 13:18-19 when He said, "Hear then the parable of the sower. When anyone hears the word of the kingdom and does not understand it, the evil one comes and snatches away what has been sown in his heart. This is the one on whom seed was sown beside the road."

God revealed words of the kingdom to me—dreams that seemed too impossibly good to be true. Instead of letting them be sewn deeply into my heart, I held them out as bait for our enemy. It's clear that when God wants to do something big in someone's life or the surrounding lives, the enemy will do anything or use anyone to try to stop it from passing. He will even go as far as taking the innocent lives of babies as casualties. It happened in Moses' and Jesus' life, and it happened in mine.

I used to tell my husband, who at the time only wanted three kids, that we had to have at least five kids because I was the fifth. I rationalized that I wouldn't be here if it weren't for my parents having five. Yet after three hard pregnancies and natural births, I told him we were done. Of course, we then both flip-flopped our stances, and he didn't know why we should stop. Yet, no matter what I did, it didn't seem like I could lose the weight from my pregnancies or the complications that developed from them.

When God spoke to me again, I sensed that I would have two more babies—a boy and a girl. It was such a strong feeling that I felt like stopping myself from getting pregnant would hinder these beautiful souls God wanted to bring into the world. God had revealed some things about my past pregnancies before and even a friend's, but nothing like this. He had specific words that I wrote out about their lives while there was nothing but a speck of hope that I would ever even have them. I was so out of my mind and so enraptured by the experience that I honestly felt like I was going to meet my Maker soon and needed to share with those who wouldn't understand my going. Hence the openly sharing on a blog post that happened. Clearly, if I was, these two kids wouldn't be brought forth into the world. I'm so glad that God didn't give up on me because of my immaturity.

Not long after, I got pregnant. For the entirety of the pregnancy, I was extremely sick and unable to hold anything down just like my first pregnancy. Only this time, I had three other kids who were five and under who didn't understand why I was so sick. As a result, we watched natural birthing videos almost daily while tears would stream down my face, and I would explain how worth it the pain and experience were because of them. It had my oldest saying she never wanted to have kids and my second oldest saying he would voluntarily go through the pain for her if he had to because they wouldn't be here if I hadn't gone through it. It was such a precious time and sweet misunderstanding that I will never forget.

Into my eighth week, I was lying on the couch when I started bleeding heavily and was in a lot of pain. Frantic, I went to the doctor only to find out I had a cyst that ruptured. I was relieved when I got to hear my baby's strong heartbeat for the first time. I felt the same relief that I had with my third when I found out my bleeding was from two subchorionic hemorrhages but still resulted in a healthy baby. They said I had another cyst, but even if it ruptured, with my baby's strong heartbeat, they thought I had nothing to worry about. Nevertheless, they told me to come in if the bleeding continued or I had any other pain. I also found out my sister-in-law and I were due the same day and shared the happy news with her and others.

Throughout the night, I felt like I was having another painful back labor and even passed what seemed like a big clot of blood. Yet, the entire time, I kept telling myself it was just the other cyst rupturing and that my baby was ok. When I went into the hospital the next morning to hear that I passed my baby the night before, I had never felt so empty or heartbroken in my entire life.

A friend of mine who has dealt with far more losses than I have, prayed over me. As she was praying, she said how we know that God didn't take my baby's life and that it was the enemy. My entire body started convulsing as I wept out loud. I don't know if I had realized that before she prayed. I was traumatized after how strong that pregnancy felt so early on, how sick I was, and then the loss of my baby's heartbeat after feeling so relieved hearing it for the first time. I was ok with not having any more kids before I felt like God promised me two more. I had only anticipated this pregnancy because of Him. I just didn't understand how He could even allow it. Feeling rejected by so many in my church and now this felt like too much to bear.

A week later, I got some devastating test results from a blood draw that had me wondering if I would ever even be able to have kids again or even live a long, healthy life. To say that everything within me felt shattered is about as accurate a statement I could come up with. This time, I didn't feel like sharing the news. I didn't know who to turn to besides my husband who hadn't the slightest idea how to comfort me. I just felt utterly alone with my disappointment. That day, I got a call from my sister several states away. When she was in the shower, she had this crazy feeling that Satan was trying to kill me. It was so strong she was crying and praying the entirety of her shower and wanted to see if everything was ok. A week later, I received a Facebook message from a friend's mom from high school who wouldn't have known what all was going on but shared this:

> Sweet Rachel, when I was driving to work today, a wave of grief rolled over me. As I asked God what it was, He said, "Pray for Rachel and for her broken heart." So I spent some time in prayer for you. Remember how much God loves you and is your comforter in this time of loss.

Later, we went to my in-laws' church, which was a few states away, where another lady prayed for my broken heart as well. Each time someone prayed over me or shared God's heart for me, it felt like a little salve was put on my open wound. The walls I had built around my heart started to crumble as God beckoned me to trust Him with my future.

Despite the results that I was already severely anemic before my ruptured cysts and miscarriage, I continued to bleed for 75 days straight with no answers from the medical community. I cried every single one of those days as I had this hope that God not only heard them but was collecting them.[3]

As God used these sweet people to sow truth and love into my heart, it helped me realize that even now, God was for me and still had my best in mind. I didn't understand why He allowed my baby to die, but I understood that God didn't want to leave me with a broken heart. He so badly wanted to sow His seeds and shine His light into my brokenness. I couldn't reap with joy until I had sown with tears[4] and allowed my sorrow to break up the hardened soil of my heart.

SON-SHINE THROUGH

I saw the sky today
All colored dark and gray
Hung over me, a cloud of gloom
Is my day doomed?
Or should I anticipate a brighter day?
I cried out to You today
But I didn't hear Your reply
I invited You with me today
But You didn't show
Why do You wish to remain silent now
When I need You so?
Am I deaf and blind?
Where did You go?
Didn't You know I needed You today?
Will it always remain this way?
Am I holding out for a brighter day
With false hope?
And if that were true
That I'll go my days without You
Please don't take me through
'Cause I need You
And I miss You
And I can't make it without You…
Please come back soon
'Cause I'm waiting for You, Sonray
To shine through these clouds of gray
And I need You to shine through
But, no matter what,

> I'm not giving up on You
> So please come back soon
> I'm in need of Your brighter view
> And how can You decline
> A request for a little Sonshine,
> When You wish to shine through?

OFTEN, when we go through hard times, we automatically assume that means that God is no longer for us. We have a tendency to try to push against our disappointments and anger or bury them. However, when we do deny our emotions, we are likely to build up resentment and bitterness that doesn't allow anything good to spring up in or from our lives. I've learned that brokenness is not something to fear, avoid, or shy away from but rather to sow into. It's a necessary part of growth. God wants us to draw near to Him in our brokenness so He can sow seeds that will produce good fruit in our lives and the lives of those around us.[5] God will never despise or turn away a broken and contrite heart.[6] When we cast our disappointment and cares on Him, we can be sure that He'll use those tears for our good. He wants to break up the hardened soil in our hearts that insists we know better and surrender our will to the One who has our best in mind and makes all things new.

As I surrendered my will to God, I learned how to release some of the burdens I had been carrying that weren't producing good fruit. In the next chapter, I hope to help you do so as well.

Reflect:

WHEN BAD THINGS happen in life, who do you blame? Why?

. . .

DOES your view of God change when He allows you to go through pain?

Do you believe that when the Bible says God doesn't want anyone to perish,[7] He only meant eternally?

Do you believe that God is for you? Why or why not?

SECTION V

SURRENDER

RELEASE

"When you release expectations, you are free to enjoy things for what they are instead of what you think they should be."
Mandy Hale

"Expectation feeds frustration as it's simply an elusive form of control by attempting to grip the reins that aren't ours to hold. Breathe. Release. Let go. Allow your life to naturally, quietly unfold."
Victoria Erickson

"To forgive is to set a prisoner free and discover that the prisoner was you."
Lewis B. Smedes

As someone who struggles with perfectionism, I often set myself up for disappointment when things seem to come up short of the way I envisioned them in my head. The loss of my baby's life was no different. The anticipation and heartbreak of that pregnancy and the more recent health news had me wondering if I was even capable of having another healthy pregnancy, which crushed my spirit. I was too broken and exhausted to shake my fists at God, but inside I was so incredibly hurt and angry that I might as well have. I felt so betrayed. The only reason I anticipated and expected a healthy pregnancy in the first place was because of a vision He gave me. I knew beyond a shadow of a doubt my expectation came from Him.[1] I just didn't understand how God could show His love for me only to let me down so hard.

God might have given me the expectation that I was going to have two more babies. However, like Jesus' disciples, I thought I knew what that would look like. Like them, I truly didn't understand until He made it come to pass later. I realized I often work so hard to make things happen and mold things into my understanding that I get disappointed when my expectations aren't met. God was trying to get me to stop leaning on my own understanding and trust the One who holds my whole world in His hands.

With each tender word God had the women who prayed for me speak to my heart, He let me know that He is a God who sees.[2] He would never forget me,[3] and He had every intention of reviving my heart and spirit.[4]

As I realized God was still good and His heart was still for me, I started to trust Him again. I realized in this life I may never truly understand why my baby had to die, but I could lean on the One who held the future.[5] As I began to surrender my will to Him, I learned the truth that Adolfo Perez Esquivel shared: "We know we cannot plant seeds with closed fists. To sow, we must open our hands."

God started showing me all the areas in my life I still tried to hold a firm grip around, afraid that if I didn't, they might slip through my hands. He showed me areas in my marriage and parenting I wasn't trusting Him with. I tried so hard to maintain some semblance of control, trying to mold them to meet my expectations of what a good marriage and kids look like. I didn't realize how much I made my marriage and kids about me—afraid of what people might think of me if my kids behaved poorly or how embarrassed I was when my husband would choose others over me. I didn't realize how much I was hindering their growth by not allowing them messy seasons in their own lives or acknowledging that they are their own persons, not just extensions of me.

God entrusted my kids into my and my husband's care and expects us to train them. He promises that if we do, when they are old, they won't depart from what we've taught them.[6] However, it doesn't account for all the years in between where they might fall flat on their faces, and we need to be there waiting for them with loving arms like the prodigal son's dad. I can't even imagine what people said of him when his son wasted all his money on parties and prostitutes or when his older brother didn't want to celebrate his return. I'm so glad God showed us an example of a love that empties itself of embarrassment over others' expectations and poor choices and continues to love and forgive no matter what mess we create, still acknowledging us as His children.

It made me think a lot about forgiveness. I thought about the Apostle Paul who wrote almost half of the New Testament. Paul, who before becoming a Christian, would be considered a modern-day Isis member today (*St. Paul and ISIS*). Paul, who threatened to murder Christians all in the name of doing what he believed to be right. I've thought about the Christians who might have lost a brother, sister, mom, dad, child, or any other relative to the man. I wondered how they must have felt to not only see him be given the grace to convert to Christianity, but then also to be one of the most influential Christians to date. What a slap in the face it must have felt like! I think sometimes I'd skim over the part[7] that Paul wrote saying he was the chief of sinners thinking about how influential he was later on in his life without remembering his backstory. The absolute conviction he must have felt when he wrote that and his inability to possibly apologize to all the people he must have hurt. The absolute need of his to press on towards the goal[8] to win the heavenly prize for which God had called him to receive. The absolute need to continually look to Jesus[9] and move on with his life. Thankfully, we have Paul's backstory and have seen how God used it for good in his future. Christians during his time wouldn't have been given that opportunity.

Sometimes like those Christians, we're not given the opportunity to have a backstory. Often the people who have hurt us the deepest don't repent; or if they do, it's a worldly repentance rooted in manipulation just trying to get us to move on. At times, they might further injure us by saying we're too sensitive (*You're Not TOO Sensitive*) as though they didn't hurt us bad enough in the first place. Sometimes, they truly are trying to help but are looking at things from an outside perspective or with false information. Maybe they've made up their minds about us without ever taking a chance to get to know us. Maybe they continuously put us in gaslighting (*What is Gaslighting?*) situations that only further their inaccurate thoughts about who we are. I've been threatened with the truth not spoken in love. I've been repeatedly told that God won't forgive me if I don't forgive others. I've witnessed and experienced such hardness of heart that grows from being treated unjustly all in the name of God. I've wished people who hurt me so badly out of my life because I felt powerless to be myself in their presence. The hypocrisy I felt for living a double life was too much for me to bear (*Purpose*).

The greatest sins and atrocities often come from those believing what they're doing is right. The sin wouldn't have such a powerful force to enslave us (*Sin Enslaves*) if it didn't have a sense of rightness[10] about it. Lies only hold power when we believe them to be truths. I often find it crazy that Satan used Scripture to try to tempt Jesus (*Temptation of Jesus*). It just shows that truth alone is not enough. It has to be used in context and spoken in love. I think my own lofty view (*My Finite Understanding*) of myself has gotten in the way of me being able to truly forgive others sometimes. My own sense of rightness has blinded me to my hardness of heart.

Some of us have every right in the world to be angry and hurt. We have every right to end a marriage or cut off people from our lives. Sometimes it's even healthy to separate for a time, and sometimes maybe the only way others will come to their senses is if they experience the finality of the consequences of their actions.

Every person's story is so different, so entirely one's own. I could judge another's story from my own lofty view of myself and say I wouldn't handle things the way others are and think that maybe I could do a better job. Maybe I could, or maybe I couldn't. I've had such a hard time coming to a place of understanding in my own life that it's foolish of me to think I can understand another's. I have to ask God to help me see others through His eyes to not grow hurt or bitter over things done to me. Only then can I truly forgive and extend grace. I will not pretend I could do any better in anyone else's shoes. After all, I didn't walk in them. I can't possibly know how I would handle others' situations if I had. If others didn't truly think what they were doing was right, they probably wouldn't be doing those things. It's not my calling to ever be in a place of judgment.[11] It's not my place to take vengeance into my own hands,[12] however tempting it may be. I don't wrestle against flesh and blood.[13] None of us do. We can accuse all we want just like the accuser of the brethren,[14] but only God knows the heart (*18 Verses about Knowing the Heart of God*). It's my mission to try to live out of His heart towards myself and others. It's much easier said than done, but what a beautiful release it is when I do!

UNCONDITIONAL

Don't believe in your past
Don't be downcast
God has forgiven you
I have too
I always asked God to let me love and forgive like Him
So when the lights fade away and it grows dim
You're just teaching me
To love unconditionally
I won't bring it up, if you don't want me to
I won't shout it out, if it hurts you
You've trusted me to tell truth
Pain exposed, I wish to soothe
I don't believe in what you were
The thought didn't even occur
The love I have for who you are now
Takes away every thought of doubt
I said I'd be there for you, my friend
And that's how it will always end
Your past doesn't make you
He has made you new
I will always love you
No matter what you do

As Desmond Tutu said, "Forgiveness says you are given another chance to make a new beginning."

A FRESH START

Today's a new day
A fresh start
But this spirit of fear
It won't let me be a part

It brought with it
An unsound mind
Weakness, hate, apathy
Weren't far behind

Now I'm suffocating
Gasping for air
Choking on these "truths"
That might not be there

This bitterness and unforgiveness
This poison I swallow
Acting as though I don't have
A choice in who I follow

Blinded and deceived
By my enemy
Shooting arrows to kill
From the side he wants me

You came to give sight to the blind
To set captives free
But I'm deprived by the lies
Fed to me

But this is why You came
This is why You died
You know what it's like
To hurt inside

Your flesh and blood
You allowed to be beaten
You sacrificed life to redeem years
The locusts have eaten

I give up these lies
I surrender my pride
I'll do whatever it takes
To join the other side

I'm making the choice
To release this bondage
These lies, this unforgiveness
That's been holding me hostage

Because tomorrow's a new day
A fresh start
I conquer these fears
I want to be a part

I'll take up my cross
And follow You
I'll forgive those who
Know not what they do

I REALIZED that before God could bless Jesus, Joseph, and Job, every single one of them prayed for their enemies who at times might not have even realized how their actions affected others. When we release our judgment and need for revenge or even just our expectations into God's hands, it is as though we are softening the hardened soil of our hearts that hinders anything from growing there. As we do, the blessings start to come, and life can begin again. As Marianne Williamson said, "The moment of surrender is not when life is over. It's when it begins."

Reflect:

ARE there any areas in your life that you're not surrendering to God? Why or why not?

Do you trust that God is good and has your best in mind? If not, why not?

ARE there people in your life you want to get even with? If so, who?

I WANT to challenge you to start praying for those people you might have listed above. Prayer is powerful. It has a way of softening our hearts and helping us release our burdens to a God who cares for us.

BELIEVE

"'If you can'?" said Jesus. "Everything is possible for one who believes."
Mark 9:23 (NIV)

"What you believe, you receive."
Gabby Bernstein

"Blessed is she who has believed that the Lord would fulfill His promises to her!"
Luke 1:45 (NIV)

I knew God to be good, but I didn't know what to expect anymore. After bleeding for 75 days straight, it finally stopped, but then it started up again two weeks later. I was devastated. I took my three young kids to the library to take my mind off of my disappointment. On our way out, the only movie on the adult shelf caught my eye—"A Winter's Tale." I didn't know what it was about, but I had a strong impression I was supposed to get it. I put one of the kids' library movies on our TV and sat at our counter so I could keep an eye on them with my own movie on our laptop—something I had never done before.

To my surprise and humor, the movie had Will Smith playing Lucifer who was trying to stop a guy's dream and destiny from happening. While there was no mention of God—only the universe—I prayed God would speak to me through it as I often do. The end lines caught me off guard, and I found myself sobbing all over again.

> "Why would so many things conspire to save one little girl's life?
>
> But what if it wasn't just Abby?
>
> What if she is no more or less special than any of us?
>
> What if we are all unique...and the universe loves us all equally?
>
> So much so that it bends over backwards across the centuries...for each and every one of us. And sometimes, we are just lucky enough to see it.
>
> No life is more important than another.
>
> And nothing has been without purpose. Nothing.
>
> What if we are all part of a great pattern that we may someday understand?
>
> And one day, when we have done what we alone are capable of doing...

we get to rise up and reunite with those we have loved the most...forever embraced.

What if we get to become stars?"

— (*A WINTER'S TALE*)

TO MY AMAZEMENT, my sweet two-year-old who could barely talk and still struggles to be understood had come up to me when I was crying and reached up her arms for me to pick her up. As I did, she so clearly said, "You're pregnant."

She'd never said that word before. I asked her to repeat herself as my mind raced through everything that had happened over the past two-and-a-half months.

She so clearly responded, "You're pregnant," all over again before wanting to be put back down to hang out with the other kids.

I had just read part of a book the night before that pointed me to Matthew 10:41 that says, "He who receives a prophet in the name of a prophet shall receive a prophet's reward." I didn't necessarily think that my two-year-old daughter was a prophet, but I knew Acts 2:17 and Joel 2:28 said that in the last days, our sons and daughters would prophesy. Even more, I knew that God could speak through anyone. I texted my husband and sister just in case, and then I saved the text on my phone as a reference in case anything ever came from it.

As God reminded me of His goodness, I felt a gentle beckoning to trust in His faithfulness all over again like I did as a child. I felt God wanting me to not only hold onto His promises but remind Him of them. In doing so, I reminded myself. God is a good Father who wanted me to believe in Him and take Him at His word, and He promised me another son and daughter. Matthew 7:9-11 NIV says, "Which of you, if your son asks for bread, will give him a stone? Or if he asks for a fish, will give him a snake? If you, then, though you are evil, know how to give good gifts to your children, how much more will your Father in Heaven give good gifts to those who ask Him!"

I knew God to be a good Father. I had no choice but to abide in Him for my next breath those days. I felt utterly alone at that time in my life. His words and promises were now tucked safely in my heart. As my daughter spoke what seemed such impossibilities at the time, I felt everything within me yearning to believe that the impossible was possible again.

John 15:7 NKJV says, "If you abide in Me, and My words abide in you, you will ask what you desire, and it shall be done for you."

I knew that I met those requirements. Likewise, I knew that God wanted these two children for me just as much as I did. There were just too many crazy "coincidences" that happened that confirmed everything I had felt God spoke to my heart. I began to loosen the tight grip I thought I needed to have to make things happen as I entrusted my situation to His care. I stopped my mind's constant need to rationalize how impossible it would be to have a child (or rather, two future children) given my current circumstances. Instead, I focused on taking God at His word and the possibility He was speaking through my unintelligible youngest daughter to get my attention. Sharing and saving that text on my phone was just a sign of how much I believed that the tiny seed my daughter planted into my heart could come to fruition. God was asking me if I would walk with Him into the unknown and trust Him every step of the way.

DAILY SUSPENSE

Each day's a daily battle, of will I live or will I not?
Will I let my continual struggle bring my weary bones to rot?
Each day I feel I'm giving up another glimmer of hope or two
Then I realize what effect it must be having on You
All along You've been telling me, "Just put all your hope,
all your trust in Me,
And everything will come together, just be patient
and you will see"
You see how hard I struggle to completely trust in You
And then I realize just how much pain
I must be putting You through
You already have my whole story written out
And You wonder why after only one chapter
I'm already filled with doubt
And then after reading the book all the way through
I look back and wonder how I could have ever
begun to question You
I have only finished reading the first chapter or two
And I have yet to see the suspense
You're gonna put me through
But the end wouldn't have such a great ending...
without the beginning
So I'll keep reading the beginning
knowing I have a lot to look forward to
And I'll keep putting my hope and trust only in You

ONLY WHEN WE surrender our will to God and believe Him at His word can He produce what's truly beautiful in and through us.

Reflect:

Is there anything God has spoken to you or prophesied over you that still hasn't come to pass? If so, what?

I encourage you to abide in God and take Him at His word. Don't be afraid to remind Him of those things. His answering of those prayers might not look like your expectations, but they always fulfill our heart's desire far more than anything we could ever produce.

BLOOM

"If we remain afraid and closed off, we'll never know what it feels like to bloom."
Lori Schaefer

"The flower that blooms in adversity is the most rare and beautiful of all."
Disney's *Mulan*

"But blessed is the one who trusts in the LORD, whose confidence is in Him. They will be like a tree planted by the water that sends out its roots by the stream. It does not fear when heat comes; its leaves are always green. It has no worries in a year of drought and never fails to bear fruit."
Jeremiah 17:7-8 (NIV)

Not long after my two-year-old told me I was pregnant, I found out I was. I don't know if it was just due to having a miscarriage before, but the entire pregnancy, I felt like I was under attack spiritually and mentally. At twenty weeks pregnant, we found out I had complete placenta previa. We prayed, and at the next ultrasound two months later, we found out the placenta moved completely out of the way. Not long after, I found out my baby was in the breech position. We prayed again, and he fully turned. I had so many crazy dreams while I was pregnant with my son that others would confirm by speaking the same exact things over him.

While I still don't understand them completely, I had no doubt that this baby was meant to be and that God has such a great calling on his life. Such a bittersweet thing it is to know that if our other baby hadn't died, our lively son that we can't imagine life without wouldn't be here. He wouldn't have even been a consideration.

In one strong push, his head came out. In a second push, the rest of his body shot out too. None of my other babies have ever been in such a hurry. It was as though he was on a mission to redeem one of the most tragic days of my life. Exactly a year to the day of my miscarriage and one day short of nine months from when my two-year-old told me I was pregnant, our sweet little rainbow baby came into our lives and reminded me once again that God had every intention of fulfilling His promises to us. Our lives would have had so much less color if he weren't in it. I also must mention, God gave us our sweet baby girl a couple years after our son. Our son and daughter that made our family complete were only a small seed of hope planted inside of me years before.

Now, when God shares His promises with me, I try not to presume I know what they'll look like or the turns that will be made along the way. I try to keep my mind and heart open to His adventurous ways. I have no doubt that we will someday meet our beloved baby, and that He's been taking such good care of her. I can't say for sure that she was a girl, but I had a feeling I was to name her Kara Michelle, which means "beloved one who is close to God."

THERE HAVE BEEN SO many times in my life that I've questioned why God allows bad things to happen to good people. I've wondered why He allows such messy, dark seasons in people's lives. However, I'm constantly reminded that no beautiful tree or plant has ever bloomed without springing through dirt. There is no lasting beauty without depth.

Psychiatrist Elisabeth Kübler-Ross shared this:

> The most beautiful people we have known are those who have known defeat, known suffering, known struggle, known loss, and have found their way out of the depths. These persons have an appreciation, a sensitivity, and an understanding of life that fills them with compassion, gentleness, and a deep loving concern. Beautiful people do not just happen.

Ecclesiastes 3:11 NLT says, "Yet God has made everything beautiful for its own time. He has planted eternity in the human heart, but even so, people cannot see the whole scope of God's work from beginning to end."

When I would read the story of the fig tree that Jesus cursed to wither and die after it didn't produce fruit in an off season, I never understood it. Now, I look at that same story and see Jesus making a promise to us. Even in those off seasons where we have every excuse not to produce fruit with our lives, with God, all things are possible. Not every season will look the same, but we can always be in the process of being fruitful, and we should never despise small beginnings.

If you're in a trying or messy season where you feel that there's no hope, please know that these dark seasons are part of the process to bring forth life. Let God sow His seeds into your brokenness and take responsibility in choosing to soften the soil of your heart because He will always be faithful to finish the work He started in you.[1] God is not looking for a beauty that fades. He's looking for eternal beauty, and that takes time to bloom.

BEAUTY'S JOURNEY

The journey,
How You wish to lead me
Transcends my understanding
Yet life is so demanding

Your ways so holy
Sometimes unravel slowly
But if beauty came fast
How long would satisfaction last?

Oh God, time seems so unkind
So we settle for the quickest find
Going on a journey
You're not leading
Hoping it will meet our every need
Disappointed, left empty

We all have needs we want to fill
And sometimes ignore that's in Your will
But beauty doesn't come without patience

Whoever heard of a hero without struggle,
without endurance?

And how much would freedom cost
If it was never lost?
Or being stress-free
If you never had a worry?

And beauty wouldn't be so rare
If you found it everywhere
And winning wouldn't be so great
If it was everyone's fate

So when this journey seems tough
And I think I've had enough
I'll continue on with patience
Remembering You have me in mind
Beauty comes with endurance
And that's what I long to find

JUST AS GOD sent a rainbow to remind Noah and his family that He would never flood the earth again, God gave us our rainbow baby to remind us He always keeps His promises. So often the stormy seasons in our lives have us wanting to give up, but that's when God wants us to surrender our hearts and will to Him, push through, and bloom.

WEATHERED HEART

You left your heart open
For far too long

Thought it was invincible
Couldn't be more wrong

You didn't use an umbrella
To shelter it from rain
You didn't know storms
Could weather so much pain

Now you're left
With a torn, weathered heart
You've tried to mend it some
But it's easily torn apart

And your heart
Once thought to easily survive
Is just dying
Dying to stay alive

In an attempt to
Rescue itself from more pain
It closed itself up
To shelter floods of rain

And the door of your heart
Was shut to many-a helpful knock
And in order to survive
It would have to unlock

It would have to open up
To see blue skies again
And it would need to let the Son
Take the place of sin

It would have to risk dying

In order to survive
And it would have to open up
If it ever wanted to thrive

And with one last gasping
Breath of air
It cried out with strength
You never knew existed there

It cried out for mercy
It cried out for grace
It cried out for healing
To take place

It cried out for forgiveness
Of not opening up before
When the Helper chose
To knock on its door

And it opened up
Wider than ever
It chose to risk everything
If it was its last endeavor

And the floods came
And the rain
But it wasn't like ones before
It washed away the pain

And the Son came
He helped your heart thrive
And with His help
Your heart will always survive

> You leave your heart open now
> Never to close
> Sometimes storms may come
> But they leave with rainbows

As God likes to turn the messy seasons of our lives around, we can dare to live.

Reflect:

Are there any seasons of your life that seemed so hopeless that God used to show His faithfulness?

If you are in a seemingly hopeless season right now, I want to encourage you to take the steps mentioned in this and the past three chapters and trust the process. If you have a journal, this would be a good time to write out prayers to God as you cast your cares upon Him. I have no doubt you will see His faithfulness if you abide in Him and His word abides in you. God never fails to keep His promises. Just remember, His ways are not our ways and His timing doesn't always line up with ours.

SECTION VI

Freedom

DARE TO LIVE

"Do not fear death, but rather the unlived life.
You don't have to live forever.
You just need to live."
Tuck Everlasting

"She is clothed with strength and dignity, and
she laughs without fear of the future."
Proverbs 31:25 (NLT)

"The thief comes only to steal and kill and destroy. I have come
that they may have life, and have it in all its fullness."
John 10:10 (BSB)

---

*S*omething seemed to shift in my mind when I realized that God is for me again. Even more so when I believed that He really would keep His promises to me. Somehow, one of the worst things I ever endured led to some of the things that brought me the most joy. It gave me courage to know that whatever I faced God would be with me. It didn't mean things would always be easy or that God wouldn't allow me to go through hardships again. However, it meant that even if I did, it had no bearing on His love for me. I didn't need to let fear of the unknown keep me from living or take up any space in my mind. The only guarantee that life gives is that death is inevitable. As a Christian, I know that death will bring me something far greater than this life ever will. When I come to the end of my life, I want to know that I lived it to my potential, not shrunk in fear.

WRITER and theologian C.S. Lewis wrote this:

> In one way we think a great deal too much of the atomic bomb. 'How are we to live in an atomic age?' I am tempted to reply: 'Why, as you would have lived in the sixteenth century when the plague visited London almost every year, or as you would have lived in a Viking age when raiders from Scandinavia might land and cut your throat any night; or indeed, as you are already living in an age of cancer, an age of syphilis, an age of paralysis, an age of air raids, an age of railway accidents, an age of motor accidents.
>
> In other words, do not let us begin by exaggerating the novelty of our situation. Believe me, dear sir or madam, you and all whom you love were already sentenced to death before the atomic bomb was invented: and quite a high percentage of us were going to die in unpleasant ways. We had, indeed, one

very great advantage over our ancestors—anesthetics; but we have that still. It is perfectly ridiculous to go about whimpering and drawing long faces because the scientists have added one more chance of painful and premature death to a world which already bristled with such chances and in which death itself was not a chance at all, but a certainty.

This is the first point to be made: and the first action to be taken is to pull ourselves together. If we are all going to be destroyed by an atomic bomb, let that bomb when it comes find us doing sensible and human things—praying, working, teaching, reading, listening to music, bathing the children, playing tennis, chatting to our friends over a pint and a game of darts—not huddled together like frightened sheep and thinking about bombs. They may break our bodies (a microbe can do that) but they need not dominate our minds.

I once thought that God seemed a little harsh when after all Job had gone through, He said to "take it like a man." However, when that story pops into my head now, all I can see is God on the sidelines encouraging Job by saying, "You've got this!" Job's circumstances were no surprise to God, and the trials Job went through were deliberately because God bragged about Job's righteousness in the presence of our enemy. God believed that no matter what Job went through, he would make it through on the other side. God ultimately had more faith in Job than Job had in himself. When we are in Him, God promises that what Satan means for evil will be used for our good and always attaches a blessing at the end. God wanted to get self-pity out of Job's head. He wanted Job to rise up with courage. If Job stayed in his self-pity, it wouldn't matter how God blessed him in the end. He would remain in the past, feeling wronged by God, his wife, and friends. He wouldn't be able to fully enjoy the blessings God brought about the rest of his life.

I've found that so often in life, we get stuck. There can be years or even decades where it might seem that we don't move forward. We remain in bitterness, unforgiveness, religion, and shame. When we feel paralyzed as a result of things that happened to us, it's so easy to take on the role of a victim—as I know from experience. Yet, any area we act like a victim in will not bring us the victory God has for us. When He tells us to "man or woman up," it doesn't mean that He lacks compassion for the pain we went through. It means He doesn't want us to dwell there, constantly reliving it.

Conversely, we can get held on a pedestal we worked so hard to build—a picture of ours or other people's dreams and feel incapable of being real with others. We put a box around God, others, and ourselves. We do the same for our dreams, visions, and happiness. When we do that, we struggle to get past whatever box we've built for those things, and our lives become crippled with fear of the unknown. We become the person playwright Eugene O' Neill shares about in *The Great God Brown*: "Why am I afraid to dance, I who love music and rhythm and grace and song and laughter? Why am I afraid to live, I who love life and the beauty of flesh and the living colors of the earth and sky and sea? Why am I afraid to love, I who love love?"

I've learned that when we take away the limits we've put on God, others, and ourselves and treat ourselves as the spiritual beings that we are, our lives become full of possibilities. We become full of wonder again, able to live life as though we were seeing it again for the first time. We're able to experience life in all its fullness, like children, and enter a world that so many are incapable of.[1]

We're able to live and let live, being led by the Spirit, and free of judgment of others because we realize that we too were once in the dark—possibly not that long ago. We live with the realization that we are starting to see God in all His wonder for the first time, and that it will take an eternity to really know Him —or even to know ourselves and what we're fully capable of. If we're too busy watching and judging others, we lose time and opportunities to truly live ourselves.

THE SECRET TO LIFE

We watch movies on the silver screen
And oh the people we steal their scene
Because we think they know what it's like
To feel alive
Everyone's dead around us now
Turn on the TV to feel somehow
Because with that fame, they must know what it's like
To thrive

But with the silence
I feel the violence
Of an enemy
Trying to make us forget
That with the stillness
And with our wholeness
And by His strength
We can uncover the Secret
To being alive

We watch others to find our role
And the emptiness of a God-sized hole
We think we can cover up
The leak
But if everyone just looked around
It wouldn't take long 'til it was found
We've lost His Strength
That makes us weak

Our busyness
May cover up the emptiness
For a little while
But with the smile
Of a little child
You'll find the vile
In a world
Trying to poison our souls
And you'll find we've swallowed it whole
When you look at our goals

But with the silence
We can fight back with violence
An enemy
Trying to make us forget
That with our stillness
And with our wholeness
And by His strength
We can find the Secret
To a life
That's lived alive

IN ONE OF my favorite passages in the Bible, Paul wrote to the men of Athens in Acts 17 starting in verse 22 and going through 31:

> I perceive that in all things you are very religious; for as I was passing through and considering the objects of your worship, I even found an altar with this inscription:
>
> TO THE UNKNOWN GOD.
>
> Therefore, the One whom you worship without knowing, Him I proclaim to you: God, who made the world and everything in

it, since He is Lord of heaven and earth, does not dwell in temples made with hands. Nor is He worshiped with men's hands, as though He needed anything, since He gives to all life, breath, and all things. And He has made from one blood every nation of men to dwell on all the face of the earth, and has determined their pre-appointed times and the boundaries of their dwellings, so that they should seek the Lord, in the hope that they might grope for Him and find Him, though He is not far from each one of us; for in Him we live and move and have our being, as also some of your own poets have said, 'For we are also His offspring.' Therefore, since we are the offspring of God, we ought not to think that the Divine Nature is like gold or silver or stone, something shaped by art and man's devising. Truly, these times of ignorance God overlooked, but now commands all men everywhere to repent, because He has appointed a day on which He will judge the world in righteousness by the Man whom He has ordained. He has given assurance of this to all by raising Him from the dead.

When I changed the narrative of my life and realized God can do and use anything, including me—giving me the reassurance that the same Holy Spirit that raised Jesus from the dead lives inside of me—I started being able to truly live. I didn't have the same fear of the unknown anymore. The future started looking full of possibilities and adventure.

In Him, we truly live and move and have our being.[2] We cannot do it apart from Him or of ourselves,[3] but when we move in the Spirit we were created to move in, we live in a world that makes impossibilities possible—a world that brings dead things back to life. A place where a glorious God wants us to share in His glory and help us realize that everything that He has is made available to us.

God doesn't allow us to go through the hard things because He has anything against us. He wants us to know that even if we go through hard things, we can move on and be unstoppable. If we live in fear of possibilities that could happen in life, we aren't living the abundant life He promises us. He wants us to be able to walk in freedom from fear, becoming fully alive in Him.

FULLY ALIVE

Let go of your doubt
True faith equals fact
Life will go on without
Time you take to react

The clock won't stop ticking
And your busy days won't get easier
The wrinkles will keep coming
And your heavy loads won't get lighter

But you can let them go
Drop them off here
Come into His presence
Let go of all your fears

24 hours a day
7 days a week
You can spend them wasting away
Or finding the Joy you seek

So cast off all your burdens
Come into His rest
Live life really living
Not always second-guessed

No "what-ifs" now
No settling for second best
Let Him pump His life into your blood
Like the rhythm of your chest

So stop your fake living
So stop living dead
You're not fully alive
'Til you let Him in your head

Reflect:

Is there anything in your life causing you to not move forward? If so, what is it?

Are there any lies attached to that thing that is causing you to feel stuck? What are they?

What are some truths that counter those lies?

When we realize that the only way lies hold power is if we believe them, we come to realize that we are often the only ones stopping ourselves from moving forward.

What will it take for you to realize you can do all things through Christ who strengthens you[4] and move on in your life?

ARISE AND SHINE

"Arise, shine; for your light has come!
And the glory of the Lord is risen upon you.
For behold, the darkness shall cover the earth,
and deep darkness the people;
But the Lord will arise over you,
and His glory will be seen upon you.
The Gentiles shall come to your light, and kings
to the brightness of your rising."
Isaiah 60:1-3 (NKJV)

"Our deepest fear is not that we are inadequate.
Our deepest fear is that we are powerful beyond measure.
It is our light, not our darkness that most frightens us.
We ask ourselves, 'Who am I to be brilliant,
gorgeous, talented, fabulous?'
Actually, who are you not to be? You are a child of God.
Your playing small does not serve the world.

> There is nothing enlightened about shrinking so that other
> people won't feel insecure around you.
> We are all meant to shine, as children do.
> We were born to make manifest the
> glory of God that is within us.
> It's not just in some of us; it's in everyone. And as we let our
> own light shine, we unconsciously give other
> people permission to do the same.
> As we are liberated from our own fear,
> our presence automatically liberates others."
> -Marianne Williamson

I've always had this strong desire to become all I was created to be and lead by example. However, my view of women and ultimately myself had been tainted and limited by the environment I grew up in and the people my life was surrounded by. I thought to please God I must be gentle and quiet, not drawing any attention to myself.[1] As an artist who loves color but an introvert that hates attention, I already held the tension of wanting to express myself with the fear of standing out.

Further, I was led to believe my body and outspokenness were shameful. The ways I sat or laid down when trying to get comfortable were always called out as a temptation—the last thing I could have ever possibly wanted. The more attention I got, the smaller I felt I needed to be. I learned to diminish my womanly attributes and all the things that set me apart as a woman to appease the critics. My womanly figure didn't feel like the crown of creation; it felt dangerous and taboo.

I got the impression that my worth was linked solely to what was beneficial to man, as I was "created to be his helpmeet." It seemed to be tied to the value I added to men's lives and what they deemed to be appropriate and acceptable. I felt it was my job to please. It didn't help that I always had men trying to give me a "voice of reason" for my "illogical," more intuitive insight. My thoughts and opinions didn't seem to hold the same weight as theirs. My judgments weren't considered valid unless they agreed with the commonly held beliefs for women. They reasoned that only men needed respect and a woman only love, as though love could come without admiration and respect.

It always amazed me that Deborah could be spoken about as a leader, but only with the explanation that there were no available men. Her situation was an exception when men didn't step up as leaders despite it saying she was a prophetess[2] and judge beforehand (*Deborah and the "No Man Available" Argument*).

I heard about Miriam getting leprosy for speaking against Moses.[3] However, I never heard about Miriam being a prophetess[4] and leader of Israel.[5] Of course, a big deal was made about women needing to be kept silent in the church and asking their husbands questions at home, though it was one small part of a letter[6] sent to a church in a culture that worshipped women and usurped the authority of men (*The Prominence of Women in the Cults of Ephesus*).

Likewise, I never heard anything positive about any other female leaders in the Bible that didn't fit in the box women were put in. While the Bible says in Christ there is neither male nor female, and that we are all one in Him,[7] I was led to believe my sensitivity and femininity were somehow second-class. I was taught to remain submissive and silent, letting my husband lead me.[8]

It baffled me that women could be worship leaders on a platform and homeschool teachers that led our sons. Yet, at some age, our sons would be taught to disregard what we have to say since women weren't supposed to teach anyone besides other women. I wondered what age my sons' thoughts would hold more value than my own. Similarly, I was taught to submit to my husband, but never heard of the need to submit to each other.[9] When I brought it up, it was always under the notion that it was only talking about submitting to other peers. Yet in Malachi 2:13-16, God was angry with the passionate men of God whose cries He ignored because they betrayed and deceived the wives of their youth. He said their wives were their companions that He made one with them from the beginning. When I looked up the word "peer," it had the word companion and talked about equal status with a person. Somehow the church has gotten the notion that women's sensitivity and distinction as a "weaker vessel"[10] has somehow made us less than the men in our lives. In looking that verse up, I realized that husbands are warned again that if their wives aren't treated with respect as fellow heirs of the gracious gift of life, their prayers will be hindered. It's no wonder there are so many dead churches around without signs that follow believers.[11] Unfortunately, despite the Biblical explanation, I've yet to hear that argument among the many excuses given that don't line up with Scripture.

In addition, I recently heard a very prominent figure in the church making light of a woman enduring verbal and emotional abuse or being smacked around once. His own words were, "If it's not requiring her to sin but simply hurting her," she's still required to submit to her husband. It has always amazed me how concerned the church is in putting women "in their place" and fulfilling their roles while seemingly dismissing the roles of men. I have a big problem when leadership is more preoccupied with putting the weight of responsibility on the woman and her reaction or submission to a dishonorable man than calling out guys who are putting women and children in danger.

While I agree that submission is a heart attitude and one can submit to a position of authority even when that authority is evil,[12] attitude is often a reflection of leadership. I don't know one woman who wouldn't appreciate and submit to a good man unless she's been incredibly hurt by men in her life. Men who are following God do not put women and children in danger. God advises a man to love his wife as he loves his own body and take care of her,[13] to provide for his household,[14] and not provoke his children to wrath.[15] I can't think of one man who would be ok with being smacked around or abused or who would take looking at porn lightly if the roles were reversed. There seems to be a connection between a man's inability to separate the shame of lust and pornography and his ability to wholly enjoy a woman. Until a man can see his wife and women in general as equal beings deserving of respect and not just made for his own gratification and fulfillment, there will always be a justification to objectify women and a dissatisfaction in intimacy.

No matter how many verses I read about Christ in us or that God's image is reflected within males and females,[16] I couldn't ever picture Christ in me as a woman. There was a blockage in my mind from so many years of listening to others' interpretations of Scripture. As a result, I missed so many other beautiful truths in the Bible that God had about women or that God shared about Himself. My inability to see Christ in me as a woman was hindering my ability to see God in all His fullness. I couldn't see or experience the softer, more feminine side of God.

Perhaps the most eye-opening revelation I had in the last couple years was seeing God's matriarchal side. In all my years of studying the Bible, reading countless Christian books, and hearing innumerable Biblical teachings, I had yet to even consider He had one. I often forget that God is not limited to gender like we are. I had such a hard time grasping that thought, and even exploring it made me feel uncomfortable thinking I might be accused of heresy. Yet multiple times while reading, it was as though God wanted me to explore this feminine side of Him. I had often heard God to be a man of war,[17] but I had yet to hear God as a mother. However, during this season I saw the side of God that gathers Jerusalem's children together as a hen gathers her chicks under her wings.[18] I read about the part of God that spreads her wings and catches and carries us like an eagle that stirs up her nest and hovers over her young.[19] I saw the promise to comfort Jerusalem as a mother comforts her child.[20] I read how El-Shaddai, one of God's many names, can also be translated to mean "many-breasted God" or "mighty breasted God."

I was reading about the foolish woman and the woman of wisdom in Proverbs 8 in The Passion Translation only to read a footnote that said this:

> Wisdom is personified throughout the book of Proverbs. Lady Wisdom is a figure of speech for God Himself, who invites us to receive the best way to live, the excellent and noble way of life found in Jesus Christ. Jesus is wisdom personified, for He was anointed with the Spirit of wisdom. (See 1 Cor 1:30; Col 2:3; Isa 11:1-2.)

In over three decades of life, I don't think I had ever heard of Jesus personified as Lady Wisdom, but it now makes sense why it would say in Proverbs 8:22 how "in the beginning I was there, for God possessed me even before He created the universe." I read on in verses 30-31 where it said this: "I was there, close to the Creator's side as His master artist. Daily He was filled with delight in me as I playfully rejoiced before Him. I laughed and played, so happy with what He had made, while finding my delight in the children of men." It reminded me of Zephaniah 3:17 (NKJV) where it says, "The Lord your God in your midst, the Mighty One will save; He will rejoice over you with gladness, He will quiet you with His love, He will rejoice over you with singing."

As God started expanding my vision on the many facets of His personality, I started being able to see myself in a new light. I was in the middle of doing something with my kids one day, still somewhat thinking about my newfound revelation as I recalled my favorite Christmas book called *Papa Panov*. It beautifully tells a story that gives a picture of Matthew 5:25 NIV that says, "For I was hungry, and you fed Me. I was thirsty, and you gave Me a drink. I was a stranger, and you invited Me into your home."

As I was dwelling on that verse, I had a glimpse of this old homeless man in "Bruce Almighty" that later turned into Morgan Freeman—who plays the role of God in the movie for those who haven't seen it. As soon as the image came to me, Morgan Freeman turned into me. My eyes welled up with tears, and I ran into the other room to thank God and write in my journal for such a glimpse. As much as I have always sought to be like God and please Him with my life, I never felt like I could truly reflect Him as a woman. Being shown only the patriarchal side of God, I feel like that gift is so often denied to women. This gift that a woman who fears the Lord could ever reflect His/Her image. It was one of the greatest gifts God gave me this past year, yet it still seems so foreign to me that I have to remind myself of it, as though it was just a silly dream I had.

From years of listening to the lies of broken men only able to compartmentalize women or getting unwanted attention even while fully clothed, I started seeing beauty and other women's sexuality as dangerous. Beauty is powerful, but powerful and dangerous are not synonymous. The beauty of a sunset speaks of the hand of its Creator just like the beauty of a woman who seeks to give God the glory. While I believe my sexuality should only be known within the protective parameters of marriage, it is also powerful, good, and healing. It is a testament that God wants us to be fully known, seen, and enjoyed by another who cares enough about us to spend his life caring for us. It speaks of a God who not only said His creation of woman was very good, but He rejoices over us with singing, takes great delight in us, and loves when we are wholly known and loved. Perversion means devoid of truth. Some men and women are so broken, they can only see others for a small part of who they are. The perversion and danger are not in a woman's beauty or sexuality. It lies in the fact that no broken woman will ever make a broken man whole; no sexuality outside of the protective boundaries of marriage will ever be without shame.

God makes everything beautiful in its time. If I am here at this time, it is my time to accept myself and others wholly for who God created us to be. When I don't, I am not just putting down myself, but I am speaking out of a false humility and saying what I think about myself is more important than what God says about me. I am saying my worth has less value than the high price He paid for it. As I see myself wholly through God's eyes, I can wholly see others too and clothe myself not out of insecurity or comparison but in the strength, dignity, and confidence God has clothed me in and allow others to do the same.

Since opening up my mind to the realization that there's so much more to God than I could comprehend, I've been easing up on myself too. I started resisting the notion that I need to be a certain way to please God and embracing the full spectrum of who He's created me to be as a woman. Instead of trying to prove that I'm capable of doing everything just as well as the men in my life, I've started embracing what sets me apart as a woman and the strengths that come through my femininity and sensitivity, and further, what I alone can do. In high school, I wrote a poem where I had started coming to terms with my humanity.

MANNEQUIN

I knew a girl once who did the
greatest impression of a mannequin.
Her plastered smile was always appealing,
And her painted mask always just right.
Well, I saw her recently
And her plastered smile was revealing
The chipped glue underneath.
Her smile was no longer plastered anymore.
Her face paint was smearing with tears
she'd never met before.
As a mannequin, she had never been so broken,
But she had never felt so real in her life.

A few years ago, I decided to make a piece of art with it. It was the first time that I did a piece of art just for the mere pleasure of it in a long time. Dealing with rheumatoid arthritis had stopped that pleasure long ago. It wasn't to fulfill any need—an assignment, art contest, our house, or any other person—just for me. I dabbled with materials I had never worked with, got lost in the music with my ideas behind it, and just enjoyed the whole experience. I was proud of myself.

While I enjoy realistic fine art that looks nice, there's something powerful about art that isn't as pleasant to look at that draws me. Expressing myself in that way felt freeing, and I felt like it matched the poem.

I had recently joined a local art group that I was excited about. People there asked opinions all the time or just shared their work that I loved viewing and complimenting. I had a question about my piece and how to capture it on film, so I thought I'd ask which angle they thought I should use. Instead of answering my question, I was told how I should study another person's artwork who combined art with poetry and express myself more like them and just critiqued harshly. Out of over a handful of comments, only one person even answered my question. The interaction left me feeling like maybe I should scrap my painting I once felt proud of and start over or replicate someone else's art. I've never been one to study others' art too much unless I'm trying to figure out how to do something because I want to keep it entirely my own.

I learned something that day. I felt like God was asking me why I allow other people's opinions to hold more merit than my own. Why do I allow other people's voices to be louder than that of my Creator's? Why would I ever try to be someone other than myself when God thought the world needed one of me too? I'm the only one who can share my small puzzle piece of Him. It's absolutely frustrating to come to the end of a big puzzle and be missing the last piece no matter what piece it may be.

Putting oneself out there will always be intimidating. Stepping outside of comfort zones will always be uncomfortable. Being vulnerable and expressing oneself always requires at least a small act of bravery in a world that seeks to make clones of us all. There will always be people trying to cut down to size anyone who stands out or those outside of the arena who critique those inside. Their criticisms are more of a reflection of them than they are of the person they're criticizing. I admire those who challenge themselves, so why can't I be one? Why can't you? As William Wallace in Braveheart says, "Every man dies, not every man really lives."

We are not mannequins. Crying is a sign of life upon arrival. Emotions show our humanity. We are not meant to watch life pass us by or try to be someone other than who God made us to be. We are not meant to stay hidden or buried. We are meant to grow and blossom, rise and shine. We are meant to step inside the arena. As a body of believers, we were never meant to stay underground, but rather be a church set on a hill that cannot be hidden. We were meant to let our light shine.[21] Our piece of His puzzle might look different than all the others,[22] but it needs to be put on the table before it can be used.

Reflect:

WHAT IS it you bring to the table that you alone can do?

DO you ever find yourself changing who you are or acting unlike yourself to appease the critics?

I OFTEN HAVE to remind myself that those who feel the need to comment on how I should live my life are rarely living a life I would want to emulate. There's a reason I'm not asking them for advice.

Paulo Coelho shared, "Everyone seems to have a clear idea of how other people should lead their lives, but none about his or her own." Usually, the people I want to glean from are too busy living their lives to comment on mine, and I have to ask them to graciously lend their time to me.

Eleanor Roosevelt shared, "Great minds discuss ideas; average minds discuss events; small minds discuss people."

Don't let small minds cut you down to their size. We were made to reflect the glory of God.[23]

UNITE

"And over all these virtues put on love,
which binds them all together in perfect unity."
Colossians 3:14 (NIV)

"It is not our differences that divide us. It is our inability to
recognize, accept, and celebrate those differences."
Audre Lorde

"The beginning of love is the will to let those we love be
perfectly themselves, the resolution not to twist them to fit our
own image. If in loving them we do not love what they are, but
only their potential likeness to ourselves, then we do not
love them: we only love the reflection
of ourselves we find in them."
Thomas Merton

I knew marriage was going to be hard, but part of me thought my love was strong enough to overcome the challenges we faced. My, did I have a lot to learn. The day my husband and I came back from our honeymoon, we had our first and last physical fight—in his parents' house. Our second reception was to happen the next day. I felt our marriage was over before it had really begun. I wondered what on earth I had gotten myself into, but I was sure to mask my disappointment in front of a large crowd of mostly strangers to me.

I had never in my life ended a relationship where I didn't still care for the other person in some way. In fact, I struggled so badly with ending relationships whether fit or not, that after the first one I ended, I prayed I'd never have to do it again. I never understood how people could go from loving a person to hating them, until I got married.

I think the only thing that kept my husband and I together in those early years was the fact that we're both stubborn. We had absolutely no clue what it meant to truly love someone. Early on, I went through all the motions of a great wife, but there was a part of me that despised him. All the while, he thought we were "fine" as I buried my disappointment deep inside and was sure to meet his expectations. On several occasions, it'd creep up to the surface, and I would lash out my anger, leaving my husband to think I was mad.

I rationalized my anger for years as he struggled with various sins and selfishness that affected me greatly. I felt completely justified in my bitterness, always keeping a track record of his growing list of wrongs. When others would praise my husband in public, I was sure to berate him so they wouldn't feel as "deceived" as I was and to get back at him for all the hurt that he'd caused me in secret.

In retrospect, I think I felt the need to justify and blame

someone for my becoming someone I couldn't stand to be around. I still struggle at times with this all these years later. His issues and our completely opposite nature brought out mine with overwhelming clarity. I hated who I was when I was with him. I didn't have the same problem with others. So I pinned it on him. He was the toxic one in our relationship, I told myself.

Neither of us truly understood the concept of being "naked and unashamed," exposing areas of each other's weaknesses to shame the other. We used areas of vulnerability as weapons against each other, feeling justified by our hurt. We competed against one another instead of acting as teammates. He valued tradition, history, logic, and competition while I valued creation, heart, truth, and honesty. His undermining of my attributes caused me to feel the constant need to perform. He's competitive by nature, but I allowed my insecurity and need to prove myself to tear him down just the same. We acted as though our attributes were superior to the other's rather than equal but different. Our differences drove us apart as we insisted upon our own ways and ideas being the right ones. We continually tried to mold the other to our image, or what we deemed to be ideal.

For decades, I prayed that God would use my life to bless and love others whose actions seemed unlovable, yet the second I was given the perfect chance, my love grew cold and thin. I think it was easier for me to love others at arm's length. I had never allowed anyone to get as close as my husband had where I could feel such heartache. Marriage felt hard and painful. It made me understand why people get divorced, have a trial run as leverage, or want nothing to do with it at all. For the first time, it made sense to me. I started looking at weddings and stories about happily-ever-afters with such cynicism. I toughed out our marriage and often tried to make the most of it, feeling blessed by the precious lives that came through it. However, marriage felt like it was my cross to bear, and there were so many times I felt I couldn't bear it any longer.

Things would seem to be getting better, only for me to stumble upon one more thing that would start our never-ending toxic cycle all over again, feeling like nothing ever changed. I felt completely stuck. I didn't want to be in a relationship without any health or growth. My husband insisted on us sticking it out, but he made little-to-no effort to bring us closer together. His only effort seemed outward, as he sought others' attention that drew us further apart. Almost a decade in and coming to terms with some of my own issues, a couple close incidents happened that left me wondering if I would ever truly be able to trust my husband.

For the first time, I felt like God gave me the choice to end it if I didn't feel like I could ever soften my heart towards him. My husband didn't see me as an equal and constantly undermined the weight of his actions, always shifting blame onto me. Yet, despite feeling like God was offering me the choice and feeling that He understood and grieved in my heartache, I still felt that it wasn't in God's perfect plan for us. I knew God cared deeply about my husband just as He did for me, and that separating what God joined together would hurt His heart too. As I visualized my husband all alone, an intense compassion for him came over me, as God gave me a sense of His heart for us.

At that time, God gave me a beautiful vision of marriage. If we could learn to truly love another whose actions are unlovable, then we could share a beautiful picture of His unconditional love for the church. I felt this warning that even if I were to leave, if I were to remain bitter or divisive and continually bring my husband down, our kids, who are comprised of both of us, would feel ashamed of part of themselves. As a result, they'd learn to hide or hate that part in themselves and others. In doing so, I would be like the foolish woman tearing my own house down.[1] It would clothe us with violence spoken about in Malachi and break God's heart who loves us both without compromise. Instead of feeling stuck in an unloving marriage, I felt this glorious grace and freedom that empowered me to want to stay and walk out this vision. I had this strong feeling that God would take care of me, making up for any area my husband lacked in, and had so many reminders of how He had been so faithful to take care of me then.

For the first time in a long time, I was able to walk up to my husband not with any hardness of heart but rather a softness as I trusted God to fulfill His promise to me over our marriage. I told my husband that even with his actions, I still loved him. I didn't plan on getting back at him. I was better than that. I wasn't going to divorce him. I let him know that if he didn't love me, I wouldn't seek it elsewhere. God had overwhelmingly shown me His love for me in my love language at the time, and I knew that even if my husband didn't, I would be ok. We both teared up.

At the time, I had let go of a lot of expectations of what God's fulfillment of His promises would look like. I had been wrong before. Things didn't happen right away as is often the case. We're both still a work in progress. However, there have been so many days that I have felt blown away by what God has done and absolutely undeserving of my husband and his goodness these days. We're learning to stop insisting that our ways of thinking are the right ways, and we're both learning that our differences give us an advantage when paired together with equal value.

I teared up as I wrote this and thanked God for not giving up on us, for how good He's been to us, and for my amazing husband who took all five of our kids on a trip to his parents' house four hours away so I could have a free birthday weekend to write and relax. Once I moved out of the way and stopped demanding my rights, God was able to show the miraculous power of His love.

So many of the problems we encounter in marriage seem to stem from the power struggle to see our differences as good things. We insist that our traits are superior to the other's. We misunderstand marriage and the way love works. We keep trying to mold others into our image or into an image we find acceptable and appealing rather than celebrating our differences and valuing them equally. God is not looking for two alike people. He is looking for people whose opposites complement each other. God wants us to submit to one another out of reverence for Christ.[2] We don't need to see the same way; we just need to have the same goal.

As we reach towards oneness in Christ, trying to model His love for each other and using our giftings together, we will model the glorious picture of Christ and His love for the church and the beautiful byproducts that come from it.[3] We need to leave room for the other person rather than trying to mold them into our own image. We were both created in the image of God and we need to respect and celebrate our differences. We can all learn from each other. We need to keep our ears open to listen rather than speak. We need to keep our heart open to understand rather than enforce our own understanding. We need to keep our eyes open to see each other through God's eyes rather than the limited view we have of each other. We need to open our mouths to speak words of life over the other rather than judgment.

Love never forces itself upon another. It always hopes, always believes, and never fails to change us and the way we see others. Love softens the soil of our hearts, changes the environment, and paves the way for growth and miracles to happen when combined with compassion. It never enforces itself upon the objects of our love. They have to choose to let it and Him have its way.

As our pastors pointed out, the goal of marriage is not happiness but oneness. Marrying for love is no more noble than marrying for sex because marrying to *get* love rather than *to* love are two entirely different things. The goal of marriage is to represent Christ and His love for the church. He wants us to come together as one and multiply that love through Godly offspring. However, when we seek oneness, we often find happiness.

As God began to redeem our marriage, I realized that any second spent not loving each other is only wasted time.

EVERY WASTED SECOND

You talk to me, mentioning
All the mistakes that I've made
The last thing I need to hear
Are all the times that I've strayed

I wish I could take back
All those painful memories
I wish I could say sorry
In a way you believe

I wish to be forgiven
Through all my mistakes
We need to cast an Anchor
Whenever our world shakes

You're right to be mad
You're right to accuse
But every second we waste not loving
Is a second we lose

I want to love you
In the good, the bad, the in-between
I live to want you
When you're nice and when you're mean

I need to hold you
In the times you want to leave
I'll give you a reason to smile
When all you can do is bereave

I want to be loved
In the good, the bad, the in-between
I live to be wanted
When I'm nice and when I'm mean

I need to be held
In the times I want to leave
Give me a reason to smile
When all I can do is bereave

Can we move forward now?
Not dwell in the past
Every second not loving is wasted
And the years go by so fast

During some of those really hard years, I found some beautiful truths in Scripture that I had somehow missed and hope will encourage others who are struggling.

1.) God is a witness in marriage.

There have been so many times in my marriage I felt utterly alone. So many times, I just wished someone could know what I've gone through or why I reacted in different ways. There were times I wished I could tell my story with the guarantee that neither of us would be judged or told that we have no hope. I used to read Malachi 2:13-16 and focus on the reason God made us one- to produce Godly offspring. Then I read it and realized that the only men who would cover the altar of God with tears are passionate men of God and that marrying a Christian man does not guarantee a woman will be treated well as so many women have come to know. However, recently, I noticed this beautiful promise in the midst of all of it. God is a witness between a man and his wife. Even if nobody else sees or knows what you've gone through, even when it feels like you're going through hell or God is distant, He is a witness; and frankly, He's not happy when women are betrayed or deceived. He hates it when we're treated unequally as He made us one. He hates it so much that He will ignore the offerings and cries of such men.

2.) Loving those who don't reciprocate your love will benefit you.

Anyone can love someone who loves them. It's not hard. Loving when it's not easy, when it seems like your love is being wasted on someone who doesn't value you is hard. When you show mercy and love without expectation, your reward will be great and you will be children of the Most High, who is kind to the ungrateful and wicked.[4]

3.) Marriage is "the Lord's holy institution which He loves."[5]

Marriage is God's idea. He gets to set the parameters for it. When done correctly, He loves it. When it's broken up, He hates it.[6]

4.) This one is probably a given, but God is Love.

When we learn to love, we become more like God.[7]

・ ・ ・

As we learn to love, God can use us to partner with and collaborate with Him. I'll share my thoughts on that in the next chapter.

Reflect:

What is the goal of marriage for you?

If you're married, is your marriage built on oneness or do you compete with each other?

Are there power struggles in your marriage? If so, can you identify them? Where do you think they come from?

Can you pinpoint any areas your love is lacking? If so, what are you going to do about it?

SECTION VII

POTENTIAL

24

COLLABORATE

"For we are co-workers in God's service; you are God's field, God's building. By the grace God has given me, I laid a foundation as a wise builder, and someone else is building on it. But each one should build with care. For no one can lay any foundation other than the one already laid, which is Jesus Christ."
1 Corinthians 3:9-12 (NIV)

"The Holy Spirit is a helper, not a doer."
Pastor Alexander Klimchuk

When I found out God could use me, it changed my life. I was the youngest attendant at church camp, only allowed to go because two of my older siblings were going. I missed the cut off by about eight months. As the youngest in my family, I didn't feel like I could make much of an impact on anyone. At one point, I nervously prayed and spoke out loud and two older girls told me how much it inspired them. When these girls I looked up to said something I did made a positive impression on *them*, everything within me felt like it might burst at the seams. The whole time, I was uplifted by them, but they shared they were encouraged by *me*. As someone who needs to feel capable and wanted, being able to work with and bless God and others in return for the things done for me is *almost* as great of a message as Him loving me.

I always felt called to bless and serve others. I thought it meant living a perfect life, free of any flaws. However, if my life happened the way I imagined it, my influence would be incredibly limited. If the things in my life happened merely because of things I had done, I might be able to take the credit. Furthermore, I wouldn't be of much help to others who are struggling if I was so far removed from their stories.

Religion would have us believe that we're supposed to wait around for God to do everything for us, or the equally disempowering message that what we do won't make a difference. Or perhaps a more dangerous message that our failures or weaknesses can't be used. The problem is, we all fail and we all have weaknesses. If we believe those messages, we'll get hung up on them and not move forward.

God wants the struggles we face to mold us and purify us so we can reflect the Lord's glory. The fact that everything we go through can help others or bring us closer to Jesus gives purpose to our pain. God is not looking for spoiled children who cannot be used. God is looking to strengthen us through our trials and tests so that after we walk through them, we will have a testimony in the end to help others along the way. Revelation 12:11 NKJV says, "And they overcame him by the blood of the Lamb and by the word of their testimony, and they did not love their lives to the death." While the blood of the Lamb cleanses us from our sins, we also need the word of our testimony to help us overcome and not shrink back when faced with death. There is no testimony without a test. Further, the testimony of Jesus is the spirit of prophecy.[1] What God has done for one, He wants to do for another. By us sharing our stories, we can help another overcome in his or hers.

I used to think that I should passively wait around and pray for God to answer my prayers or show up in different areas of my life. Lately, I've had the sense He's been asking and waiting for me to show up. Sometimes I feel the need to remind myself that I have the Holy Spirit living in me. If I show up, so does He. Maybe He's just waiting to co-labor or collaborate with us, and He's waiting on us to do our part in showing up so He can work through us. He wants to breathe His life through our lips. He wants to serve others with our hands. He wants to show the bigger picture through our art, visions, and prophecies. He wants to travel to distant lands with our feet. He wants to serve through our hands. He wants to speak life through our tongues. He wants a body that edifies and encourages each other. In 1 Peter 4:10-11 NIV it says this:

> Each of you should use whatever gift you have received to serve others, as faithful stewards of God's grace in its various forms. If anyone speaks, they should do so as one who speaks the very words of God. If anyone serves, they should do so with the strength God provides, so that in all things God may be praised through Jesus Christ. To Him be the glory and the power for ever and ever. Amen.

God isn't looking for a damsel in distress. He's looking for a bride who makes herself ready.[2] He is looking for sons and daughters who rise up and do what Jesus did.[3] Christ in us is the hope of glory.[4]

JESUS IN US

To father the orphan
To visit the widow
To love the child with chocolate-brown eyes
That no one seems to know

To give hope to the hopeless
Sight to those without vision
To offer peace and love
Was that not Christ's mission?

But sometimes I think we don't realize
We're the only Jesus some get to see
So I pray He opens up our eyes
And helps us realize
That's our reason to be

We could be the answer to a child's prayer
We could be the ears that listen,
The heart that wholly hears
The hands that give
And the time that shows He really cares

We are to be Christ's hands
We are to be His feet
To tread upon near and distant lands
Proclaiming Christ has won the victory

So let's allow Christ to use us
To show He still exists
We could be the only sign of Jesus
That shows who He really is

WE EACH HAVE a part in showing Christ. We are each called to be His hands and feet or various parts of His body. In the body of Christ, God has given us each gifts and abilities that are all needed.[5] I've found when a church is operating in a healthy way, giving a place for each person and their gifts, everyone feels like a part of the body. People are a lot happier and look for solutions to problems that arise as they feel they can contribute to them. When people's gifts and callings are neglected and they feel rejected, they see those same problems with overwhelming clarity and won't look for a solution as they don't feel like they can contribute. They wait around for God or others to do the "lifting." It's incredibly sad to go into churches that don't value members and their gifts and whose ministries bring about division in the body of Christ rather than unity.

Ephesians 4:11-16 NIV says:

> So Christ Himself gave the apostles, the prophets, the evangelists, the pastors and teachers, to equip His people for works of service, so that the body of Christ may be built up until we all reach unity in the faith and in the knowledge of the Son of God and become mature, attaining to the whole measure of the fullness of Christ.
>
> Then we will no longer be infants, tossed back and forth by the waves, and blown here and there by every wind of teaching and by the cunning and craftiness of people in their deceitful scheming. Instead, speaking the truth in love, we will grow to become in every respect the mature body of Him who is the head, that is, Christ. From Him the whole body, joined and held together by every supporting ligament, grows and builds itself up in love, as each part does its work.

I realized I cannot find who I am until I know which role I play in the grand scheme of life. Mahatma Gandhi once said: "The best way to find yourself is to lose yourself in the service of others." Billy Graham said, "When we come to the end of ourselves, we come to the beginning of Jesus." Jesus said He did not come to be served but to serve and give His life as a ransom for many.[6] So many greats have seemed to come to the same conclusion that Jesus said in Mark 8:35, "For whoever wants to save his life will lose it, but whoever loses his life for My sake and for the gospel will save it."

I found when I made my identity about myself, I lost all sense of who I was. When I made it about Him and others, I found who I am and what I'm called to do.

IDENTITY

Lost behind a wardrobe of faces
A new mask for each setting
If none seem to fit quite right
Is there one that I'm forgetting?

When the crowds change with the seasons
And society determines who's to fit in
Who do I run to when I'm all alone
And I don't know the One within?

When I'm feeling empty,
And loneliness screams louder than the music I blare
When my heart is bleeding and my soul is dying,
Where do I place my fear?

When my hunger is insatiable
Always left incomplete
Do I ever really conquer
When left feeling utter defeat?

If I do the things I don't want to
And don't do the things I do
Is who I am determined by unfulfilled intentions
Or unintended impromptu?

If I don't know who I am
Who should I portray?
When I'm lost behind a joyful face
Does that mean I am okay?

If I'm just a character in a story
And I don't seem to fit the scene
Am I playing the wrong role?
Or am I meant to be a drama queen?

If who I am is what you see
And all the sudden I change
Is who I am what you saw before?
Or who I was, re-arranged?

If I can display who you are
But have trouble being me
Am I who I play best?
Or do I have a lost identity?

And if all You are,
Is who I wish to be
Is who I am what I display now
Or what I'd like to see?

It seems that I feel more alive
When I display You
And when I die and let You live
I am made anew

> So forget about who I am
> See who I'm trying to be
> Because who You are
> Is meant to be
> My identity

"So all of us who have had that veil removed can see and reflect the glory of the Lord. And the Lord—who is the Spirit—makes us more and more like Him as we are changed into His glorious image." 2 Corinthians 3:18 (NLT)

Reflect:

Are there any areas you are waiting on God in? What are they?

Sometimes I feel like we know what we're supposed to do but feel hesitant to do it. Did anything come to mind while reading that? If so, what?

What is it you can do about your circumstances? The next right thing if you will. Are there classes you could take? A mentor or counselor you could see? An accountability partner you could ask?

If you truly believed that the Holy Spirit lives in you and you are the living representation of Christ on earth, would your life look any different? How so?

. . .

Sometimes we do have to wait on God. Most of the time, He's not on our timetable. However, I've found it's not the passive waiting I tend to think of but an active waiting. There's usually something we can do in the meantime to prepare our hearts and join His forces. When we learn to collaborate with Him, we can change the world, or at least the portion that we live in.

CHANGE THE WORLD

"If you want to change the world, go home
and love your family."
Mother Teresa

"As the family goes, so goes the nation, and so goes
the whole world in which we live."
Pope John Paul II

"Spread love everywhere you go: first of all in your own home. Give love to your children, to your wife or husband, to a next door neighbor . . . Let no one ever come to you without leaving better and happier. Be the living expression of God's kindness; kindness in your face, kindness in your eyes, kindness in your smile, kindness in your warm greeting."
Mother Teresa

My Christian Apologetics and Hermeneutics' teacher once posed a question to my high school class. He asked, "If there was an unbeliever and a believer about to fall off the edge of a cliff and you only had the ability to save one, which one would you save?"

We all said we'd rescue the unbeliever. We knew that the believer would go to Heaven, and perhaps this would give the unbeliever a chance to make things right with God. He countered that he thinks we should rescue the believer and shared with us Galatians 6:10 NKJV (emphasis mine): "Therefore, as we have opportunity, let us do good to all, *especially* to those who are of the household of faith."

Lately, I can't seem to get that out of my mind. I wonder, like us students, how many people put those in their households on the back burner and think of extending goodness to the people in the family of God last. I think about how different the world might look if we put those in our households and in the family of God first and then extend outward. I can't help but think that those outside the church would be looking for ways to get in if we were truly known by the love that we have for one another and shared the benefits of having access to everything God has.[1]

Who wouldn't want to be a part of a loving family who always has one's back? Instead, we lack patience, understanding, love, and grace for those inside despite not knowing where others are on their journeys and save our energy to minister to those outside. As soon as someone joins, we often expect them to serve before they've really had the chance to be served. Often, we don't care to find out what the rest of our family has to offer through their different perspectives, personalities, experiences, beliefs, and even gifts assigned to them. Religion would make clones of us all and accuse anyone who doesn't look the part. Sometimes when I see the division and brokenness we've created, I wonder why anyone from the outside would ever want to join and why anyone on the inside would feel safe to share their failures or questions for fear of accusation or—*gasp* —just the appearance of not looking like we have all the answers.

Being a facilitator in our church for Living Free Ministries, I've heard and seen the impacts of broken families. It doesn't seem like anyone has come out unscathed. Some might look the part from the outside, but each family seems to have their own set of issues.

Having five kids who all have a vast array of personalities and a variety of narratives of how they translate the same experiences from earlier years in their lives has taught me a lot. I've realized how my own fears and struggles through various seasons might have hindered their growth or my own limited understanding might have shaped the very fabric of their lives. I'm so thankful that I know from my own story that God can use all the messes I've created or experienced and put them all to good use. Carrying the weight of five other human beings, or even one, is too much to bear. I'm so thankful Jesus took that upon Himself at the cross.

Looking back, I understand how my own upbringing has probably made me more independent than most. I've believed lies that I'm too much or not enough just like other people, and I don't like to be a burden. When I first got married, if something was wrong in our house, I'd research or watch videos and fix everything myself. I was so self-sufficient that it wasn't until years into our marriage that I found out my husband felt like I didn't need him because I never asked for his help. The whole time I thought I was being helpful as my dad hated the to-do lists my mom made him. My husband, however, has a hard time seeing what needs to be done but is good at getting things done, and he actually wants me to make him lists. It just shows you can't make general assumptions about anyone.

My husband, on the other hand, is the biggest family man I know. It's one of the things I love most about him. However, his inability to leave and cleave or speak up and set boundaries with his own family early on caused a great deal of hurt in our marriage and family. His prioritizing of family over me as an individual caused me to feel unwanted. He was the first one in his family to get married, so they didn't have any practice with in-laws. As a self-proclaimed mama's boy, he never saw any issues going to his mom whenever any trouble arose in our relationship and wasn't one to admit to his own faults that might have caused those problems. It didn't help that his only sister is best friends with his mom and first girlfriend. Those relationships caused a myriad of issues to arise, which didn't help the fact that the little they knew of me early on was solely based on what he shared or their perception of me from those uncomfortable circumstances. None of us had the opportunities to get to know one another outside of those situations.

As one who loves tradition and leadership, my husband had no problem telling me what I should and shouldn't do or how I should and shouldn't feel as a mom based on what he saw his own mom do growing up. When he wanted to talk or get advice —often over things we discussed and had a disagreement on or before he even discussed things with me—my husband's mother was the first one he called up. She always agreed with him about everything, and he'd disregard anything I had to say though she wasn't the one who was affected by the choices made. His lack of ownership and hatred of confrontation left room for a lot of resentment to grow in my life, and unfortunately, I swallowed Satan's bait whole.

When we got married, it didn't feel like I was gaining a family. When we'd have disagreements that were discussed as a family with them knowing so little about me besides a difference of opinion, it felt like everyone was ganging up on me. When his parents came to visit, I felt like a stranger in my own home and wondered why I was even there. I'd question why my husband chose to marry me if he didn't value my feelings or anything I had to say, didn't make room for me or how I did things, and always expected more than I had to offer. I found myself shrinking back or privately lashing out in frustration at my husband's lack of consideration for me and communication with his family. While we both grew up in Christian families, we had some polar opposite experiences and opinions. With the first grandchildren and a lot of differing thoughts on how they should be raised, there wasn't a lot of practice on what were healthy boundaries. My husband's relationship with his parents was a big contrast from his siblings'. Since they married later on, the rest of the in-laws had experiences very much unlike my own. My feelings of rejection only heightened as they seemed to be welcomed in with open arms. My offense with my in-laws only grew as I felt I was the only one on the outside who could see any of the problems within. I didn't know how to detach my actions and who I was from how I felt. I had a hard time being myself around them as my hurt and offense only grew.

The unhealthiness of my marriage, the hurt and rejection I felt, and my husband continually going to them left me feeling rejected and alone to tend to my own wounds. The toxicity of different situations and the self-pity I developed made me blind to my own issues or any good thing that came from my husband's family.

When I'd hear about decluttering the toxic relationships from one's life, of course they were always the ones I'd think of first. I felt I could be myself around pretty much everyone but them. Maybe it was because I'm a type one on the Enneagram or just the fact that I'm a woman, but I didn't know how to move on when something was amiss in my life, especially such big relationships. My bitterness and resentment towards my husband and his family and even God for bringing these people into my life always lay just beneath the surface and were affecting who I was becoming. I felt incapable of moving forward as I couldn't stop dwelling on the past and all the ways I thought I had been wronged. I didn't care about how I might have been making them feel as my anger felt justified. I'd read articles on narcissism, gas lighting, and manipulation and could see my husband and his family in all of them as that's what I was seeking out.

In Scripture, it says "seek, and you will find."[2] I learned that it doesn't just apply to spiritual principles. I read the verses about Christ coming to bring division and setting a daughter-in-law against her mother-in-law in Matthew 10:34-36 and felt like I was just going along with Scripture and further justified my stance. My hatred left me blind to my disgusting self-righteousness. To say I was hurt and offended is a severe understatement. I didn't know how to move past the walls I built,[3] and I didn't make much effort to show any love in return. I was too busy shielding myself from any sign of vulnerability or any way I could potentially be hurt.

In our "cancel culture," justification of disowning and disassociating with others is on the rise. It's getting easier to pinpoint all the ways we've been wronged and all the toxicity we've been dealt. It's only natural to read things and look at others to blame when we've been hurt. It's a lot harder to self-reflect on areas we might need to grow or accept that the people that are in our lives or the situations we are in are often there for a reason. Rather, it's easier to see everyone outside of our circle as a ministry we readily extend mercy to while we have higher expectations from those closer to us, leading to our disappointment.

When God showed His great love for me again, He showed me His love for them as well. I felt the strong foundational walls I built around myself soften as Genesis 50:20 popped into my head: "You intended to harm me, but God intended it for good to accomplish what is now being done, the saving of many lives."

It wasn't necessarily because *they* intended to harm me as

much as our enemy did. I kept directing my anger towards them and fell into the trap laid out for me by our enemy. He knew what would affect me most based on what I cared about. The closer someone is, the more the effect one has on us.

There's this part in Jonah chapter 4 where God tried to teach Jonah a lesson on mercy. Jonah ran away from God and got as far away from Nineveh as he could because he hated the barbaric Ninevites so much and knew God would be gracious to them.

It says this:

> When God saw what they did and how they turned from their evil ways, He relented and did not bring on them the destruction He had threatened.
>
> But to Jonah this seemed very wrong, and he became angry. He prayed to the Lord, "Isn't this what I said, Lord, when I was still at home? That is what I tried to forestall by fleeing to Tarshish. I knew that You are a gracious and compassionate God, slow to anger and abounding in love, a God who relents from sending calamity. Now, Lord, take away my life, for it is better for me to die than to live."
>
> But the Lord replied, "Is it right for you to be angry?"

Then God causes a plant to rise up in the desert heat and give Jonah shade. When God takes it away, Jonah gets so angry, he sounds suicidal. God asks if Jonah has a right to be angry, and Jonah insists that he does. In verses 10-11 it shares God's reply:

> But the Lord said, "You have been concerned about this plant, though you did not tend it or make it grow. It sprang up overnight and died overnight. And should I not have concern for the great city of Nineveh, in which there are more than a

hundred and twenty thousand people who cannot tell their right hand from their left—and also many animals.

It was so difficult to surrender what I felt was my right to be angry. It took so much for me to get to that place. I had to pray for them and God's will for their lives to soften my heart. I had to approach them in love and vulnerability when I felt like I might have a heart attack exposing myself to someone I didn't feel cared for me and might use what I shared against me. I had to realize that I could be powerful and keep my love on (Silk, D.) even when they might not reciprocate it. I had to learn to take care of my introverted needs and set boundaries at times because I know I can fall into the same pattern of thinking when I feel hurt by different circumstances and have to tell myself that they're not necessarily rejecting me. I had to realize I couldn't count on my husband or his family to change. I had to do the work, or it would always be an area that Satan would toy with me on when God wanted to use it to grow my love and my story to help others in similar positions and make me unstoppable.

Nowadays, we're taught to love ourselves so much that we want to cut off anyone we feel isn't loving us well. We make our stories about us, when it's about glorifying Him. When we allow a root of offense and bitterness to come into our lives, it sucks the life out of us and hardens our hearts to ever receive or give any love. Love has a high price tag, but it's worth the investment.

Love will cost your impatience, your discomfort, your hatred, your envy, and your pride. You must give up being rude, selfish, and easily angered. You must surrender your evil thoughts and perversions. You must be willing to bear things you don't like, believe and hope for things you can't see, and endure trials you wish to give into.

1 Corinthians 4:13-17 NKJV put it this way:

Love suffers long *and* is kind; love does not envy; love does not parade itself, is not puffed up; does not behave rudely, does not seek its own, is not provoked, thinks no evil; does not rejoice in iniquity, but rejoices in the truth; bears all things, believes all things, hopes all things, endures all things.

From experience, I can tell you the alternative to love simply isn't worth it. C.S. Lewis shares in his book, *The Four Loves*:

There is no safe investment. To love at all is to be vulnerable. Love anything, and your heart will certainly be wrung and possibly be broken. If you want to make sure of keeping it intact, you must give your heart to no one, not even to an animal. Wrap it carefully round with hobbies and little luxuries; avoid all entanglements; lock it up safe in the casket or coffin of your selfishness. But in that casket – safe, dark, motionless, airless – it will change. It will not be broken; it will become unbreakable, impenetrable, irredeemable. The alternative to tragedy, or at least to the risk of tragedy, is damnation. The only place outside Heaven where you can be perfectly safe from all the dangers and perturbations of love is Hell.

When I opened my heart to love again, I saw so many beautiful aspects of my husband's family that I missed when I was operating under a spirit of rejection. Some of them I noticed before but didn't perceive the same way. They want to be there for every occasion when it comes to family and spend as much time together as possible. I can count on them to want to be there for my kids and all their events. I'll get lots of pictures when we're around when I had very few growing up. When you're a part of the family, there's not much you can do to get rejected. I've seen them support and love family through messes that would have gotten me shunned from my own family until they were cleaned up.

My husband's family might not have been everything I wanted initially, but they're everything I needed. They've shown me a picture of God's love and grace I wouldn't have seen if I stayed stuck in offense. God's been teaching me to honor *all* people[4] —not just the ones who think like me or believe the things I do, but all people—Republicans and Democrats, blacks and whites, believers and unbelievers, males and females, Catholics and Protestants. Every single one of us is made in His image. Each one of us is His creation. We cannot say we love God and hate our brothers and sisters. If we can't look at the least of these and see Jesus, it's our vision that is short-sighted. Hebrews 12:14-15 NIV says, "Make every effort to live in peace with everyone and to be holy; without holiness no one will see the Lord. See to it that no one falls short of the grace of God and that no bitter root grows up to cause trouble and defile many."

I realized my vision of God has been so small and limited to only what I could see and what I was capable of representing. Yet, even if I was fully immersed in His glory, I am but a small fraction of a picture of Him. We need each other. When we don't strive to live in peace and holiness with everyone, no one sees God. When we do, we all benefit in sharing a picture of Him.[5]

AN OCEAN OF GLORY

How small did I think You are
Thinking You could fit within
The cages of my finite mind
As You break down walls again

How mighty did I think I am
To think I could understand

The fullness of Your plans
Or the outline of Your hand

How limited my thoughts
Thinking our sessions
Could grasp Your truths
Or end without questions

How wrong I've been
To think my ideas of right
Should ever be accepted
Without putting up a fight

How narrow the road
I've walked on so far
To think it's the only way
Just because You are

How vain I must be
Crossing off the possibility
That the least of these
Could ever be me

How blind my sight
How foolish to think
An Almighty God is held hostage
By my unbelief

You're calling me to step up
To see from Your staggering view
My small frame, my fear of heights
It's too great for me to do

Maybe all You wanted

Was for me to see
This speck of sand cannot contain
An ocean of glory

From the beginning, God told us to be fruitful and multiply as we fill the earth and subdue it. Family was God's idea. It was the first command He gave us, and it still rings true today. He's been using dysfunctional families and people to bring about His plan since the beginning of time. God wants to turn parents' hearts to their children and children's hearts to their parents.[6] It gives God pleasure to adopt us into His family.[7]

I heard that God made it so that when we have children and grandchildren, we learn to love ourselves more as we see parts of ourselves in these little people we adore. Unfortunately, the opposite is also true. When I was struggling to see myself the way God sees me, I kept believing lies that I would screw up my kids and would be pained when I saw any flaws of mine in them. I had such a hard time not seeing them as an extension of me. When we don't like ourselves, we're going to have a hard time seeing little mirrors of ourselves running around. Often, when immersed in the shame of religion or rejection, I think we project that onto God. However, as God's children, He sees us in Christ (*How Does God See Me*). He looks at us like He sees Jesus—the beloved, with whom He is well pleased.[8]

Studies have shown that one of the greatest things you can do for your children is to eat dinner regularly with them as a family. It really doesn't matter what the meal is, as long as the atmosphere is warm and engaging. (*The Most Important Thing…*)

One of the only traditions that has seemed to last for decades in my family is my parents' weekly spaghetti night. It has been going on for over two decades as I found that I wrote about it in an old diary at the age of twelve. Through the years, my parents have fed probably at least a hundred different people other than our immediate family during those nights. We've had foreign exchange students, old friends, new acquaintances, lonely neighbors, and extended family all come through our doors and share a meal with us.

When I was younger, my introverted-self hated that I never knew who was going to come eat. At times, I'd wished it was just our immediate family as I felt awkward having people that I often didn't know coming into our home. Yet now, it's one of my fondest memories and one of the things I hope to continue on—the whole "when you have more than you need, build a bigger table not a higher fence" idea. Having other people around kept our meals probably more civil than if they weren't there. Not to mention, now, I have friends from all over the world—some that I still contact and who feel almost as close to me as some of my family.

There seems to be something magical that happens when we share a meal together and eat with glad and sincere hearts.[9] It seems to be a bridge builder that crosses cultures and belief systems and brings people together in unity and acceptance. It creates an equal setting for those around the table. A feast of celebration was thrown when the prodigal son returned to his father.[10] David said that God prepares a table before him in the presence of his enemies.[11] It's one of the last things Jesus did on earth.[12] One of the most important invitations we could ever receive is to be invited to the marriage supper of the Lamb.[13] Meeting and breaking bread together was put on the same level of devotion as prayer, fellowship, and teaching in the early church.[14] It seems like something that should be prioritized now as well. Because when we dine, we all come together as one.[15]

WHEN WE DINE

You look at me
The sinner I am
With gazes that could kill
Any human man

Your judgmental eyes
Your "more-holier-than-thou" stare
Has it won any lost souls?
Has it gotten you anywhere?

With standards so high
You can't even live up to
You can't look sinners in the eye
Or place yourself in their down-trodden shoes

You think this is going to win them?
You think this is how God is pleased?
Didn't you know He came to save
Lost souls such as these?

What's the good news
About an unmerciful judge?
Who gives what people deserve
And will never budge

Your illustration of Jesus
Must be all wrong
Because my Jesus came to heal the sick
And show sinners even they belong

He knows we are nothing but dust
He always takes that into mind

He looks on His children with compassion and love
Of a different kind

He looks down with love
On a sinner such as me
And asks this same wretched sinner
To dine with Him and be free

He understands
This is who I am
This is me
A mere human
Lost in inconsistency

But it never stops Him from accepting
A sinner just as me
And while neither you nor I deserve it
Accept who you are, His gift, and be free

So cast down your hypocritical image
Realize you're a sinner just as I
But I'm accepted and you're accepted
When with Him, we dine

For right now He's setting up a table
For you and I
And we'll experience His grace, love, and acceptance
When we dine

Reflect:

Is it easier to extend love in your household or outside of it?

Why do you think that is?

DISAPPOINTMENT COMES FROM UNMET EXPECTATIONS. Are you disappointed with any family relationships? Do you feel anyone is disappointed with you? If so, what kind of expectations do you have for them? What kind of expectations do they have for you? If you don't know what that looks like, you might want to gently ask them, seeking to understand without getting defensive. It might be an eye opener and connector for both of you.

I'VE READ THROUGH OTHERS' advice that the only chance of keeping a relationship with a narcissist or proud person is to lovingly set boundaries and let them feel the weight of their choices before their actions destroy all health and hope in the relationship. It's one of the most loving things you can do. It says that "God resists the proud but gives grace to the humble."[16] In light of this, are there any areas of pride in your own life that God might be lovingly allowing the consequences to happen to humble you?

Do you pride yourself on self-sufficiency, or do you realize your need for God and others?

LEAVE A LEGACY

"The things you do for yourself are gone when you are gone, but the things you do for others remain as your legacy."
Kalu Ndukwe Kalu

"We all die. The goal isn't to live forever, the goal is to create something that will."
Chuck Palahniuk

"But the steadfast love of the Lord is from everlasting to everlasting on those who fear Him, and His righteousness to children's children, to those who keep His covenant and remember to do His commandments."
Psalm 103:17-19 (NIV)

I want to be remembered the way I remember my Grandma Jones. With short, white wavy hair atop her head, tan stockings to cover her soft white, hairy legs, and fake teeth she didn't always have in, a plump belly, and a jolly smile she often wore with a breezy sun dress, she wasn't the most conventionally good-looking woman. However, she was one of the most beautiful, warm souls I have ever encountered. She's always the first person to come to mind when I think upon the Maya Angelou quote: "I've learned that people will forget what you said, people will forget what you did, but people will never forget how you made them feel."

My grandma had this amazing ability to make everyone around her feel loved and cherished. She never had a lot of money. Our Christmas gifts from her were pieces of candy that I don't even recall. However, every time we visited, she'd whip up some of her delicious homemade biscuits, pancakes, and my dad's favorite banana pudding as though it was her greatest pleasure. When we were in her presence, she always made us feel like the most important people in her life and carried with her a warm smile that exuded so much grace and love. She seemed so radiant to me.

What made her attitude and warmth seem so significant though was how incredibly difficult the circumstances were in her life. She lost her teeth at the age of twenty from a strong medication she had to take. She was married at the age of nineteen to an alcoholic eleven years older than her who was abusive at times and always grumpy when we visited. They lived in a tiny box of a house with little to get by, yet I never heard her complain or act like there wasn't enough to share. She always cared about others and shared God's love with whomever she encountered. Despite her lack of earthly wealth, she was one of the most loving and fruitful people I knew, and we all remember her with such fondness.

On the other hand, I had another grandma that always felt so cold. Pictures of her in her youth made her look like a young, happy Marilyn Monroe, but by the time I knew her, it was hard to see the resemblance. My memories of her weren't nearly as affectionate as that of my other grandma. "GiGi's" husband, my grandpa, was one of the sweetest men I knew, but the two of them didn't get along at all or even sleep in the same room. When I was younger and didn't quite understand how marriages work, I remember asking my parents why my two nice grandparents couldn't be married to each other and the two mean ones together. My mom said that GiGi wasn't always that way, and that my grandpa didn't treat her that well growing up. She never seemed to move past that, and her bitterness lay just beneath the surface in her life, affecting who she was and how she treated others. GiGi's heart became hardened, and her love felt so cold. I never knew if she cared for me at all, and while we were taught to honor and respect our elders, I'm sure I made her feel the same way.

My grandparents on my mom's side were strong Catholics who never considered divorce to be an option. Nonetheless, throughout my childhood, I often wondered if it would be better for them to have separated with how hostile they seemed towards each other. Just before GiGi died, her mind completely gave way, and she became like a young child again. It was the first time I ever saw my grandparents ride in the same car together where my grandpa opened the door for her and helped her get in. I saw them hold hands as my grandpa helped her walk. I found out that her mind was unwell most of my childhood, and for that short time just before her death, I was able to experience a warmth from her I had never felt and told her I loved her for the first time I could ever remember as tears streamed down both our cheeks. Those moments gave me the answer to the wonders of my youth, and I was thankful my grandparents stayed together if only for that short time. For a brief time after, my mom said GiGi was starting to get better and considered taking care of her in our home. The thought of that terrified me as I recalled past experiences and wanted to remember her from my last encounter. GiGi died shortly after that, and I often wondered if it was my fault she died so soon.

At her funeral, the eulogy shared made me wish I had taken the time to get to know her. I wanted so badly to have experienced her in all her glory, to have known her at her best, and to have seen her overcome the hardness of life. She had done so many great, admirable things.

While neither of my mom's parents seemed the least bit wealthy, they were constantly trying to bless others. Every week, my grandpa spent his hard-earned retirement money taking his immediate family out to eat one day and his entire extended family out another. He always joined us for our weekly spaghetti dinners too, where he'd make sure to bring plasticware and butter the garlic bread. He would always joyfully say, "look at all these people who are here because of me."

Despite the little money they lived on, he made sure to leave a good inheritance to his children. When he passed, we realized what a bridge builder he was to our whole family. GiGi on the other hand, saved up money from decades of babysitting and teaching kids from her home and paid for half our tuition and our cousins' tuition so our parents could send us to a good private school among other things. They both cared so much for others. When GiGi died, I wrote a poem thinking about the legacy I hope to leave behind and thinking about how often I spend time wasted on meaningless things rather than things that are eternal.

IMMORTALITY

So immortal we pretend to be
Living life half-heartedly
Buried passion underneath
School, work, TV
And meaningless nothings
That can't even take up six feet
And while we make up an excuse
For every vanity replacing moments of life we lose
We're digging our way
To endless graves
In a cemetery we create
To fill with lost, lonely, unloved souls
To match our hearts' plentiful holes
That could have lived and been loved
If we only knew of
The fatal plague of not fully living
Takes others with us
But we have a chance
To take another stance
Be the one who dies
In order to live
In order to sprout
In order to birth new life
From death
Is that not immortal?
Is that not what we want from life?
To know that our lives
Did not just die
But multiplied
In bringing life
To those around us
Even after our time

Seeing such a stark contrast between my grandmas' reactions and their effect on me made me realize that while life would be full of trying times, I had the power to choose how I responded in life. I could allow the difficulties to harden me and make me cold, or I could let them soften me and warm my heart to others God puts in my path.

At my lowest points, I had become so concerned about how my life was affected by others, rather than how my life could contribute to others. I lacked any hope of being set free or helping another and was absolutely miserable. Our Pastor Tanya Klimchuk once said, "The difference between a happy person and a miserable person is a noble cause." I couldn't agree more. When the doctor came in shaming me for trying to take my life, I remember looking at the cold, white walls, envisioning the girl in the rain painting I had done. The thought came into my mind that others might come in for the same reason, feeling as empty as I had felt, and one of my favorite Emily Dickinson poems came to mind:

> If I can stop one heart from breaking,
> I shall not live in vain;
> If I can ease one life the aching,
> Or cool one pain,
> Or help one fainting robin
> Unto his nest again,
> I shall not live in vain.

I think coming face to face with death teaches one how to live and how to set one's priorities in order. I realized when we make our lives only about ourselves, they become so small in the grand scheme of things. Therefore, when we die, so does our impact. We can't take our wealth, fame, or possessions with us and they don't usually affect the people we love in a good way as they often fight over the possessions we've left behind. When we set our eyes on eternity and make our lives about Christ and His love, our influence lives on in the lives of others who remain after us. The gift goes on as they in turn pass it on. Our lives are not made to be lived unto ourselves; they are only a part of the bigger picture that is meant to glorify Him. When we live in Christ, our death is gain[1] and produces a harvest as the seeds we've sown multiply in the lives we've touched.[2] Our death is not the end of us. It's just a passing through to a life of eternity with Him.

So often, I think we are barely surviving to get by day to day that the thought of reaching out and extending past ourselves overwhelms us. I know that those thoughts have run through my mind during different seasons of my life where I have felt stretched thin. However, I always remind myself of a time in high school where a boy in my class affected the rest of my life with one sweet compliment.

On my way to a volleyball game, he looked at me and told me that I should be a nose model to sell tissues. It was pretty silly, but another girl chimed in and agreed—they kept talking about how much they liked my nose. What they didn't know is that when I was younger, I was always under the impression that my nose stuck up too much and made me look snobby. Neither of my sisters' noses did that, and I always thought they were so beautiful.

When I was my younger, awkward self, I'd hope that whatever guy I liked would see them and have the hope that maybe I might grow up to look like them. I remember sitting with my best friend a few times who thought her nose hung too far down, and I'd hold my nose down while she held hers up. I don't even remember if we were joking around about it or not because it was an insecurity that I really had.

As I grew older, I always got compliments on my eyes or smile but never my nose, which only seemed to confirm my thoughts. I never planned on changing it, but I believed it was one of those things I'd have to begrudgingly accept despite trying to believe God made me how He did for a reason. It didn't help that my nose was always so flat up top that if I ever tried to wear glasses, they'd always slide down or I'd have to push them up so much that they left a big indention where they were.

This boy at school not caring about how silly his comment might have sounded set me free from a life of insecurity about my nose. Even better, when I'd see the ultrasounds of all my children later on in life, their little upturned noses were the first thing I noticed that brought a smile to my face, seeing that a part of me was in all of them and not thinking of it as a bad thing. His comment might not have changed the world, but it changed mine. Ever since then, when I'm not too wrapped up with myself and all the stresses of life, I've tried to look outward. If I'm thinking something nice about someone, I try to share it with them—no matter how funny it might seem or foolish it might make me look. I hope my words set others free like his words did for me.

I've found that the more I'm faithful in the little things, God keeps calling me to greater things.[3] The more I grow and am able to manage the blessings God has already given me, the more He calls me to,[4] and the more I feel a tug that there is so much more—more of Him, more to live, more to grow, more of others—that I can reach.

Andrew Murray once shared a quote that resonates with me:

> You will ask me, are you satisfied? Have you got all you want? God forbid. With the deepest feeling of my soul, I can say that I am satisfied with Jesus now; but there is also the consciousness of how much fuller the revelation can be of the exceeding abundance of His grace. Let us never hesitate to say, 'This is only the beginning.'

God is a God of more. He seeks to multiply what we surrender to Him. He's a giver of dreams and visions.[5] So many of us are just living to get by, to fill our own tanks. We become like stagnant bodies of water when God wants streams of living water to flow from within us.[6]

For so long, beliefs, perfectionism, and fears limited me so much in my life and creativity. Yet I have found that when I remain in God and allow Him to do His work in my life, trusting Him with His process, my limits cease to exist, and my creativity flourishes. His creative genius never ceases to amaze me. When I've run into problems in my life now or even in flipping the different houses we've lived in, I've stopped trying to enforce my vision and started asking God what He has in mind. When I do, my mind is filled with ideas and some of my best work and favorite pieces have come from the most frustrating situations. Maya Angelou said, "You can't use up creativity. The more you use, the more you have." As I abide in God and remove any blockages that keep myself from being fully connected to Him, His Spirit and power flow through me and produce good fruit in and from my life.[7]

As I have come to dwell on things that are more eternal, my dreams and visions seem to continually expand. Instead of continuing to have a poverty mindset, I've started thinking more about the future. I think of who I want to serve, what kind of impact I want to have on the world, and how disappointed I would be in myself if I were to stay right where I'm at for years to come just because I couldn't overcome my fears or invest in the dreams God has given me enough to take risks. It's entirely different from the messages I heard growing up.

Surely, the love of money is the root of all kinds of evil, and many people have done very evil things all for the sake of money being their end goal. However, money is also an asset to make things happen. I think Satan wants us to fear it and not trust ourselves with it to keep Christians weak and our influence limited in this world.

As we've learned to hold out our hands to God's blessings, tithe,[8] and give to others in obedience to what we've felt God calling us to do, the blessings continue to come, our needs keep being met, and we have felt called to use our money wisely to extend its reach further. It's no longer about us clenching our fists and holding on tight to it for fear of us losing it, but rather it's about us asking God how we can use it for what He has in mind. In the end, we can't take it with us anyway.

Luke 6:38 NIV says, "Give, and it will be given to you. A good measure, pressed down, shaken together and running over, will be poured into your lap. For with the measure you use, it will be measured to you." When we make it our mission to advance God's kingdom, we tap into the resources He has made available to us and seek how our money can change the world around us to create a better place for our children and future generations. We start looking to invest and support those who have similar goals.

I realized that I don't want to limit what God wants to do through me because I allowed my circumstances to become greater than what God desires for my life. He wants me and He wants us to be fruitful and multiply.[9] To not just build our kingdoms, but His. When we don't produce good fruit with our lives, we're just wasting time and taking up space that another could be using in our stead.

In Esther 4:14, Esther's cousin Mordecai reminded her of this truth when he said, "For if you remain silent at this time, relief and deliverance for the Jews will arise from another place, but you and your father's family will perish. And who knows but that you have come to your royal position for such a time as this?"

Esther was an orphan who was forced to marry a wicked king who didn't treat her much better than a sex slave. She had to fast and ask all those around her to pray before she even felt brave enough to approach her husband for fear of her life. Even then, she was terrified and still felt the need to hesitate and look for another way to please him before she felt she found favor in his eyes.

Esther had every reason to play a victim, to shrink back in fear. She had every reason to speak badly about probably a much older husband who disposed of his ex and entertained thoughts of putting her to death simply for not wanting to expose her beauty to a palace of drunk men. He was a man who disregarded girls and women and had them at his disposal. Someone who expected purity while not caring that he would exploit theirs or give it in return. Esther had every reason to be bitter and let life happen to her.

Sometimes I think we gloss over the context of the story because we place such a high value on beauty, position, and fame. We overlook what it took for Esther to become who she was. Her cousin reminded her that if she didn't rise up and fulfill her role, God would find another way to rescue His people. She made a choice to not let her circumstances destroy her life and the lives of those she cared about. She chose to not let God have to use another person to save her people, because if He had to, He would. Her actions created a ripple effect on her people. The people of God increased, and their enemies who came against them were afraid.[10] Because she allowed God to use her and rose up in courage and wisdom, we still talk about her today. She left her mark, or signed her signature if you will, on the world. I don't know of one person—Christian or not—who hasn't heard her name despite how uncommon it is. That is what it means to leave our mark on the world.

LEAVING YOUR MARK

Like a tiny drop of water will leave the water stirred
Like a tiny sparrow will leave her voice heard
Like a candle shining in the dark
You're called to leave your mark

If a single Man can save all nations
If a song can touch a person through a radio station
If a simple smile and a warm embrace
Can stop a suicide from taking place
What is it you will do
To make an impact too?

Why are Christians in hiding?
When others, through us, should be finding
The only way to true life
Is found in Jesus Christ

So come out of your shell now
Take a step in the sand of hearts now
Let your light be shone through the dark
Now's the time to leave your mark

For others through us should find
That when it was our time to die
We left behind a mark
That led to Jesus Christ

SOMETIMES LEAVING a legacy might be just as simple as thinking about another person and complimenting them without caring about oneself as my friend did. Maybe it's intentionally going about one's days and looking for ways to bless another person. Most of the time, it comes from living in obedience to God and loving Him and others as He told us to.

Almost every Biblical character is remembered for their acts of obedience to God. Often it comes from blessing others with the gifts, talents, and possessions He's given us, or the money or resources loaned to us. Sometimes, like David writing Psalms, it's for passions pursued that still affect us today. Frequently, it's from the traditions and stories passed down from generation to generation. Perhaps it's loving and not giving up on a broken person like Jesus does and staying in what feels like a hopeless marriage to give hope to future generations like my grandparents did.[11] Maybe it looks like sharing our blessings and supporting people and causes that are important to us. Sometimes it's from showing hospitality to strangers or remembering those in prison.[12] Other times, it might just be trying to be the women God called us to be, loving those in our care, and raising the next generation to love and serve Him.

The point is, we need to reflect on our lives and figure out what is most important to us before we can ever truly make an impact on our world or in the lives of those we care about. It's not enough to just find out who we are in this life—we need to find out what we're called to do and how we want to be remembered. It's ultimately like signing our signature at the end of our lives. Every artist and art collector knows how important that is.

If we want our impact to last through generations, we need to advance a Kingdom that will have no end.[13] Our times come as no surprise to God, yet He still spoke that promise to us. When we are rooted and grounded in God, He can produce a harvest from our lives just by us living in obedience to His voice.[14] When we glorify fear, wealth, and disobedience or anything over the knowledge of Jesus Christ,[15] we are only capable of doing what we alone can do and cease to live up to our potential. If we make our lives only about ourselves and the advancement of our own kingdom, our impact will die with us. We might say we are progressing Christianity, but in reality, we are reducing it as God gives us over to a debased mind that cannot multiply.[16]

When we surrender to God and partner with Him in the re-creation of ourselves, we can rest assured that He will finish the work He started in us.[17] When we remain in Him and set our eyes on eternity, we will bear much fruit with our lives.[18] The best is truly yet to come![19] The end of our lives will be better than the beginning[20] as we are transformed from glory to glory.[21] As Marcus Aurelius shared in the "Gladiator," "What we do in life echoes in eternity."

After Hebrews talks about so many legacies left behind from people of faith in the hall of fame, it says in Hebrews 11:32-12:3 NIV:

> And what more shall I say? I do not have time to tell about Gideon, Barak, Samson and Jephthah, about David and Samuel and the prophets, who through faith conquered kingdoms, administered justice, and gained what was promised; who shut the mouths of lions, quenched the fury of the flames, and escaped the edge of the sword; whose weakness was turned to strength; and who became powerful in battle and routed foreign armies. Women received back their dead, raised to life again. There were others who were tortured, refusing to be released so that they might gain an even better resurrection. Some faced jeers and flogging, and even chains and imprisonment. They were put to death by stoning; they were sawed in two; they were killed by the sword. They went about in sheepskins and goatskins, destitute, persecuted and mistreated—the world was not worthy of them. They wandered in deserts and mountains, living in caves and in holes in the ground.
>
> These were all commended for their faith, yet none of them

> received what had been promised, since God had planned something better for us so that only together with us would they be made perfect.
>
> Therefore, since we are surrounded by such a great cloud of witnesses, let us throw off everything that hinders and the sin that so easily entangles. And let us run with perseverance the race marked out for us, fixing our eyes on Jesus, the pioneer and perfecter of faith. For the joy set before Him He endured the cross, scorning its shame, and sat down at the right hand of the throne of God. Consider Him who endured such opposition from sinners, so that you will not grow weary and lose heart.

As Hebrews shared, we are surrounded by a great cloud of witnesses watching how we will run our race and carry the baton they passed onto us. They're rooting for us to finish it well and continue the work they started in our lives. All of creation is waiting for us to rise up in our identity and partner with God in changing the world around us.[22] We cannot do that if we are stuck in bitterness, mourning our brokenness, or not coming to accept our lot in life and pressing on. We must move past ourselves and think about how God wants to use our situations to make us fruitful in the lives of others.

Ruth Stull, a missionary to Peru said, "If my life is broken when given to Jesus, it is because pieces will feed a multitude, while a loaf will satisfy only a little lad."

We are made to do hard things and conquer great challenges. We don't have to be products of our environment or victims of our circumstances. We are made to be overcomers and history makers. We are made to be fruitful and multiply. We're not just made to consume life but give it. We are life givers. It's time we show up in our lives and reveal to the world what it's been missing out on. I know that you will.

Reflect:

LIFE CAN BE TOUGH, but it is so short in light of eternity. What kind of legacy do you want to pass on? What is it you hope people will remember about you when you die?

WHAT ACTIONS CAN you take to make that happen?

SO MANY PEOPLE try to hold onto wealth or fame in life, but people are the only eternal beings on this earth. Only what we do for God and others lives on. In looking at your life, how can you use what you've gone through to help others?

JAMES 4:14 SAYS, "Why, you do not even know what will happen tomorrow. What is your life? You are a mist that appears for a little while and then vanishes."

If you knew you were going to die tomorrow, what is it you wish you had time for more of and what would you hope to pass on to your loved ones?

IF YOU DON'T SHOW up in life or get set free from the things that are limiting you, what kind of impact will that have in the lives of those you care about?

I JUST WANT you to know I have every hope for you and believe through God's Word, His gracious Spirit, and my own experience . . .

"You can rise up from anything.
You can completely re-create yourself.
Nothing is permanent.
You are not stuck.
You have choices.
You can think new thoughts.
You can learn something new.
You can create new habits.
All that matters is that you decide today
and never look back."
Idil Ahmed

CONCLUSION

Women, the world needs us, every part of us. We are gifts to mankind.[1] It needs us at rest with who we are without the performance, requirements, or expectations. The world needs us to realize the worth God has given us and the value He's placed upon us. Those unable to see us for all we are have no idea what they're missing out on. The shackles of shame might be causing us to be unaware of ourselves.

The world needs our beauty, love, and sexuality—all so powerful and made to be delighted in. Our beauty shows the handiwork of our Creator.[2] Our love is able to captivate our husbands for eternity. Our bodies are capable of satisfying our husbands all the days of our lives and equally powerful enough to be used to bring strong men down to their graves.[3] May we use them wisely.

We are royalty—daughters of the King. May we dress like it. There's a reason the world shockingly points out when there's any indiscretion[4] or lack of propriety among royalty. May we not offer our bodies to anyone who can't see us and enjoy us completely for all we are under the protective covering of God's intentions[5]—a man who vows to cherish us, protect us, and provide for us[6] all the days of our lives. [7]

If we feel the need to compete before marriage, marriage will not fix that. It only sheds light on it. A man willing to break his vow with you will have no problem breaking his vow to you. We're better than that. We are exquisite in our uniqueness—so much more than the bodies we all possess. May we not be guilty of letting such small pieces of us distract others from being able to see us for all we are. (*Bikinis Make Men* . . .) May we not seek to steal the spotlight from another woman who also should be wholly seen and loved without comparison. May we all support each other, letting our own light shine instead of trying to diminish the lights of those around us.

The world needs our fearless spirit that can talk to serpents,[8] our discernment that places blame[9] on whom it is due[10] while realizing our part in believing his lies. Any area we act like a victim in cannot produce life. The world needs the strength of our sensitivity to spread compassion in its calloused state. Out of this compassion is the place where miracles happen.[11] It needs our courage that stands at the foot of the cross when the majority of the men around us run. It needs our nurturing nature that brings life to everything we give attention to, called to be mothers of all the living before ever giving birth (*Lockyer's* . . .)—but what a blessing children are![12] It needs our insight and forbearance to not cling too tightly to the lives we need to one day let go of [13] if we ever want them to thrive. It needs our queenship to pass on the crown and make room for those we hope to be queens in our sons' lives just as we want to be given room in our husbands' lives. It needs our hearts soft and fertile to plant the Word of God inside of us (*The Soil of Your Heart*), and our dependence on the Holy Spirit to grow fruit from it.[14] It needs us to drink deeply from His bottomless well[15] and eat His bread offered daily.[16] The whole world is seeing the devastating results of what happens when we are not seen, rejoiced in, or used fully for who and what we were intended to be. God has given us the free will to parade a lifestyle contrary to and beneath the quality of life He had in mind,[17] able to be wholly known and loved for all we are (*Naked and Unashamed*), fitting together like a puzzle that's undeniably seen,[18] able to represent His image together in our totality,[19] and to multiply life (*100 Verses about Fruitful and Multiply*) without fear of disease.[20] A sharing in responsibility from men who help us see the lives we create for the blessings they are (*What Does the Bible Say about Children?*), able to receive us as the blessings we are.[21]

A woman who's unloved and unwanted grows hard and bitter. A woman not given her rightful place becomes demanding or grows callous and hides, losing her gentle nature. No good fruit grows from bitterness. Women know the devastating reality of that. It takes a very brave woman to maintain softness despite injustice, to grow life within her, and sometimes be willing to share that life with another in the hope they can produce a better environment than she can—letting go of the very heart of her she wishes to thrive. The shame a woman must feel who solely bears the destruction of a life she helped produce. May we mourn the loss of all the lives affected by such corruption. May we combat the lies that cause any human to not see the value of life with truth rather than shame, as no good fruit has ever come from shame and no potential ever grown out of irresponsibility.

I know we're hurting, and our sensitivity is said to be a weakness. I know the shame we carry from an early age that says anything done like a female is less than our male counterparts. I'm aware that being told to act like a woman but think like a man makes it seem like something is wrong with the way we process things. I've worn the straight jacket and bore the burden of responsibilities society and religion have forced upon us which often have more to do with personality, environment, and culture than anything else. I know the weight of the entire universe often rests on our shoulders, always being reminded it was the woman deceived first.[22] The man who failed to speak up knowing the truth[23] and ate as well, not acknowledged[24] despite God giving him the command in her absence.[25] I've carried the burdens placed upon us to bring life to every area of our homes even when we're running on empty with little regard to the presence of the men in our lives. (*Women Are Literally . . .*) The complete lack of respect we give men, enabling them to not bear the weight of any responsibility within the home or showing the significant importance in their roles as fathers, husbands, or co-inhabitants.

I know we've been told we're too much, that those who judge unjustly have tried to silence us[26] or those who think that one small part of a letter[27] sent to a church in a culture that worshipped women and usurped the authority of men should pertain to every woman in a church that should extend beyond four walls.[28] I know so many of us have been mistreated, betrayed, and deceived by men who cover the altar of God with tears, but God will not hear them or answer their prayers until they realize they are one with us and treat us accordingly.[29] Bullies are always intimidated by the voices of the oppressed.

Others might be good men, completely unaware of the injustices that come from women being silenced. Satan always appears as an angel of light,[30] and he hates when we join together in our authority and totality sharing a picture of Christ and His love for the church.[31] He will use anyone above us to bruise our headship.[32] Men who cry out upon the altar of God are passionate men in the church, and a church with unanswered prayers is a dead church. Dead churches can slander prosperous churches all they want, but until they look within and love us as they love themselves, they will never show a picture of Christ who loves the church and gave Himself up for her. Christ who loved us in our darkness, while we were still sinners,[33] who loved us first without our performance or submission.[34] Christ who saw women for all we are and never turned us away despite what onlookers would say. Christ who is the desire of all the nations.[35] He's still alive. There's still hope!

May we be the Esthers of our generation— born for such a time as this![36] May we stop waiting for the scepter to be extended to us first,[37] stop waiting for permission to be the queens God has already crowned us to be![38] The world needed Mary, the mother of Jesus. It needed Mother Teresa that the whole world acknowledged as a mother despite her lack of a husband or biological children,[39] and it needs the life-giving nature of us as well. The world needs the life that comes from whole women who are walking in the freedom of the Spirit.[40] We have the choice to choose life, so that we and our descendants can live.[41] Women walking in freedom, the life givers who make up over half the population and give life to those within us and all around us, can change the world for the better.

May we all be women of valor, clothed in strength and dignity, able to laugh without fear of the future[42] all the days of our lives.

May we realize the deception in a world that tries to keep us small and silent, that tells us we need to wear a mask in order to be beautiful or not look sickly. A world that would have us starve ourselves in order to fit the ideal. A world that seeks to diminish our worth, telling us our lives are purely accidental, and tries to get us to abort the very lives we helped create.

May we see with full clarity the shame brought upon us seeking to erase the very scars that show we have lived, that devalues our capacity to grow in great depths of wisdom as we age, and doesn't acknowledge the praise that belongs to a woman who fears the Lord.[43]

May we choose to live and give life to all who are around us! What a gift we possess. What a gift that we are! May we live lives that reflect that.

BIBLIOGRAPHY

100 Bible Verses about Fruitful And Multiply. What Does the Bible Say About Fruitful And Multiply? (n.d.). https://www.openbible.info/topics/fruitful_and_multiply.

18 Bible verses about God Knowing The Human Heart. (n.d.). https://bible.knowing-jesus.com/topics/God-Knowing-The-Human-Heart.

27 Bible verses about God Freeing Captives. (n.d.). https://bible.knowing-jesus.com/topics/God-Freeing-Captives.

65 Bible Verses about Sin Enslaves. What Does the Bible Say About Sin Enslaves? (n.d.). https://www.openbible.info/topics/sin_enslaves.

Bevere, J. (2018). *The bait of Satan.* Church Strengthening Ministry.

Compassion International. (2020, March 3). *What Does the Bible Say About Children?* Compassion International. https://www.compassion.com/poverty/what-the-bible-says-about-children.htm.

Dean, M. E. (2018, January 22). *What Is Gaslighting? A Sneaky Kind Of Emotional Abuse That Can Harm Your Mental Health.*

BIBLIOGRAPHY

BetterHelp. https://www.betterhelp.com/advice/relations/gaslighting-a-sneaky-kind-of-emotional-abuse/.

Dell'Amore, C. (2021, May 3). *Bikinis Make Men See Women as Objects, Scans Confirm*. Science. https://www.nationalgeographic.com/science/article/bikinis-women-men-objects-science.

Dittmer, R. A. (2019, April 4). My Finite Understanding [web log]. https://www.lifegiver.site/post/my-finite-understanding.

Dittmer, R. A. (n.d.). Purpose [web log]. https://www.lifegiver.site/post/purpose.

Eight Verses that Show Jesus Christ Lives in You. (2014, October 19). [web log]. https://blog.biblesforamerica.org/8-verses-showing-jesus-lives/.

Eve - Lockyer's All the Women of the Bible - Bible Gateway. (n.d.). https://www.biblegateway.com/resources/all-women-bible/Eve.

Fishel, A. (2019, March 1). *The most important thing you can do with your kids? Eat dinner with them*. The Washington Post. https://www.washingtonpost.com/posteverything/wp/2015/01/12/the-most-important-thing-you-can-do-with-your-kids-eat-dinner-with-them/.

Goldsman, A., Goldsman, A., Platt, M., Tadross, M., & Allard, T. (n.d.). *Winter's tale*.

GotQuestions.org. (2013, April 3). *Home*. GotQuestions.org. https://www.gotquestions.org/how-does-God-see-me.html.

Hillin, T. (2017, July 24). *Women are literally expected to do all the chores, depressing study finds*. Splinter. https://splinternews.com/women-are-literally-expected-to-do-all-the-chores-depr-1793861364.

Knowing Jesus. (n.d.). 13 Bible verses about Trance. https://bible.knowing-jesus.com/topics/Trance.

Krockett, K. (n.d.). Who Were the Pharisees. Prattville; Making Life Count Ministries.

Marg Mowczko. (2014, September 20). The Prominence of Women in the Cults of Ephesus [audio blog].

https://margmowczko.com/the-prominence-of-women-in-the-cultic-life-of-ephesus/.

Mowczko, M. (2012, June 28). Deborah and the "No Men Available" Argument [web log]. https://margmowczko.com/deborah-and-the-no-available-men-argument/.

Naked and Unashamed. Focus on the Family. (2020, June 23). https://www.focusonthefamily.com/marriage/naked-and-unashamed/.

Silk, D. (2015). *Keep your love on: connection, communication & boundaries*. Loving on Purpose.

Simon, N. (2014, December 5). *You're NOT Too Sensitive*. GoodTherapy.org Therapy Blog. https://www.goodtherapy.org/blog/you-are-not-too-sensitive-0502135.

Sophia Institute Press. (2014, September 14). *St. Paul and ISIS*. Catholic Exchange. https://catholicexchange.com/st-paul-isis.

Staff, B. S. T. (2018, April 12). *Temptation of Jesus - Bible Story*. biblestudytools.com. https://www.biblestudytools.com/bible-stories/temptation-of-jesus-bible-story.html.

Sussex Publishers. (n.d.). *Guilt = Good, Shame = Bad*. Psychology Today. https://www.psychologytoday.com/us/blog/love-and-sex-in-the-digital-age/201401/guilt-good-shame-bad.

Treat, W. by C. (n.d.). *The Soil of Your Heart*. cfaith. https://www.cfaith.com/index.php/blog/22-articles/christian-living/21152-the-soil-of-your-heart.

Woning, E. (2020, January 23). *The Lesbian in the Mirror*. Moral Revolution. https://www.moralrevolution.com/blog/the-lesbian-in-the-mirror.

INDEX OF POETRY

A
A Child's Love .... ch. 2, pp. 17-18
A Fresh Start .... ch. 18 pp. 207-208
All or Nothing .... ch. 9, pp. 101-102
An Ocean of Glory .... ch. 25, pp. 284-286

B
Betrayal .... ch. 7, pp. 80-81
Beauty's Journey .... ch. 20, pp. 220-221
Bound .... ch. 6, pp. 72-73

C
Conquering Loneliness .... ch. 2, p. 19

D
Daily Suspense .... ch. 19, p. 215

E
Enough .... ch. 15, pp. 174-175

INDEX OF POETRY

Every Wasted Second ....ch. 23, pp. 257-258

F
First and Last ....ch. 8, pp. 93-95
Fully Alive ....ch. 21, pp. 236-237

G
God Has Won the Victory ....ch. 11, pp. 119-120

H
His Story ....ch. 2, pp. 26-27

I
Identity ....ch. 24, pp. 270-272
Immortality ....ch. 26, p. 295
Inside of You ....ch. 14, pp. 153-154

J
Jesus in Us ....ch. 24, p. 268

L
Leaving Your Mark ....ch. 26, p. 302

M
Mannequin ....ch. 22, p. 247

P
Pieced Together ....ch. 16, pp. 184-185

Q
Questions of Existence ....ch. 5, pp. 61-63

R
Reduce Me to Love ....ch. 4, p. 52

INDEX OF POETRY

Ruined .... ch. 9, pp. 102-104

S

Salt and Light .... ch. 12, pp. 137-139
Son-Shine Through .... ch. 17, pp.193-194
Spiritual Makeover .... ch. 3, pp. 41-42
Stability .... ch. 10, pp. 111-112
Substituting the Absolutes .... ch. 6, pp. 73-75

T

The Least I Could Do .... ch. 4, pp. 53-55
The Lion in the Lamb .... ch. 12, pp. 129-130
The Right One .... ch. 5, pp. 60-61
The Secret to Life .... ch. 21, pp. 233-234
The Way is You .... ch. 1, pp. 8-11

U

Unconditional .... ch. 18, p. 206
Unearthed Treasure .... ch. 1, pp. 6-7

W

Warrior .... ch. 11, p. 118
Weathered Heart .... ch. 20, pp. 221-224
What's Been Done and What's to Come .... ch. 14, pp. 156-158
What's Missing .... ch. 14, pp. 161-162
When We Dine .... ch. 25, pp. 288-289
"Won" Lost Girl .... ch. 14, pp. 159-160

NOTES

1. ENVISION

1. Heb 12:2
2. Prov 29:18
3. Prov 14:12
4. 2 Cor 12:8-10

2. CHANGE YOUR NARRATIVE

1. Matt 17:21
2. Eph 1:4; Rom 8:29
3. Rev 12:12
4. Rev 12:10
5. Luke 4:18; Exod 33:19
6. Gen 50:19-20
7. Rev 12:10; 2 Cor 1:3-7
8. Phil 1:6
9. Deut 31:6; Heb 13:5
10. Rom 5:8
11. Rom 8:38
12. Prov 24:16
13. Eph 2:8-10 NLT
14. Isa 55:8-9
15. Rev 22:13
16. 2 Cor 12:9-10
17. Rom 8:28
18. Matt 5:10-11
19. Isa 61; Luke 4:18-19
20. Ps 16:11
21. Acts 10:9, 11:4, 22:17; Rev 1:10, 4:2, 17:3, 21:10
22. Matt 7:16-18
23. Matt 19:26
24. Jer 32:27; Gen 18:14; Luke 18:27
25. Rom 2:4
26. Heb 12:2

27. 1 Cor 2:9
28. 2 Tim 2:13
29. Isa 43:19
30. Job 1:6-12
31. John 10:10
32. Rom 8:30-32
33. Deut 31:6; Heb 13:5
34. Prov 18:21
35. Acts 4:11
36. Jas 2:19
37. 2 Pet 3:9
38. John 1:3
39. Ps 16:2

3. DEFINE

1. Isa 64:6
2. Rom 2:4
3. Jer 29:11
4. Exod 9:16
5. Ps 139:16-17
6. Ps 139:13
7. Ezek 16:4-8
8. Ps 139:14
9. Luke 15:11-32
10. Matt 23:37
11. Rom 8:38-39
12. 2 Pet 1:3
13. Rom 8:29
14. John 14:12-14
15. Rom 8:2
16. 1 John 3
17. Rom 8:19-23
18. Job 33:4
19. Num 22
20. Rev 19:10
21. Acts 2:17
22. Josh 2; Heb 11:31
23. Matt 11:19
24. Mark 3:22-23
25. Gal 3:28
26. John 4

27. John 8:1-11
28. Gen 3
29. 1 John 4:10
30. 1 Cor 6:9-11

4. MAKE ROOM

1. Rom 3:23
2. Eph 2:8-9
3. 2 Cor 10:5
4. Eph 6:12
5. John 3:30

5. STAY HUNGRY

1. 1 Kgs 3:16-28

6. FILL UP

1. Phil 4:8
2. Heb 12:2

7. CHOOSE

1. Rom 8:28
2. Deut 4:24

8. RETURN

1. Ps 73:25-26

9. COMMIT

1. Matt 22:37; Deut 6:5
2. Matt 4:1

10. PREPARE YOURSELF

1. Heb 12:4-12
2. Heb 5:8

11. FIGHT BACK

1. Rev 12:10
2. Phil 4:13
3. Rom 2:1
4. 2 Pet 2:10-11
5. Eph 6:12
6. 2 Cori 10:4-6

12. FREE YOUR SPIRIT

1. 1 Cor 3:19
2. Jer 17:9
3. Ezek 36:26
4. Col 2:16-23
5. Rev 22:18-19
6. 2 Cor 3:15
7. 1 Cor 2:14
8. Heb 13:8
9. Malachi 3:6
10. Rev 21:5
11. Acts 17:24
12. John 20:19
13. Gal 3:28
14. Num 22:21-39
15. Luke 1:41-44
16. Acts 2:17

13. REST

1. Matt 3:17 NKJV
2. 1 John 4:18
3. Eph 2:8-9
4. Rom 8:38-39
5. 1 Sam 15:22
6. Isa 30:15

7. Ps 46:10-11
8. Gen 1:27
9. Ps 139:14
10. John 3:16

14. KNOW YOUR WORTH

1. Ps 139:13-14
2. Jer 29:11
3. Phil 1:6
4. John 3:16

15. RECLAIM

1. Ps 17:8
2. Gen 3:20
3. Isa 54:1
4. Acts 2:17
5. Exod 15:20 ESV
6. Mic 6:4 ESV
7. Gen 1:31
8. Matt 4:11

16. TAKE CARE

1. Luke 4:16
2. Matt 4:11
3. Luke 6:12-19
4. John 11:35
5. Matt 4:4
6. John 5:19
7. Isa 54:5
8. John 14:26; 1 John 2:27

17. SOW

1. Job 42:7-9
2. Luke 1:46-56, 2:19, 2:43
3. Ps 56:8

4. Ps 126:5
5. John 12:24-25
6. Ps 51:17
7. 2 Peter 3:9

18. RELEASE

1. Ps 62:5
2. Gen 16:13
3. Isa 49:15-16
4. Isa 57:15
5. Prov 3:5-6
6. Prov 22:6
7. 1 Tim 1:15
8. Phil 3:14
9. Heb 12:2
10. Prov 14:12
11. Job 38-42
12. Deut 32:35, Rom 12:17-19
13. Eph 6:12
14. Rev 12:10

20. BLOOM

1. Phil 1:6

21. DARE TO LIVE

1. Matt 18:3
2. Acts 17:28
3. John 15:5
4. Phil 4:13

22. ARISE AND SHINE

1. 1 Pet 3:4
2. Judg 4:4
3. Num 12
4. Exod 15:20 ESV

5. Mic 6:4 ESV
6. 1 Cor 14:34-35
7. Gal 3:28; Mal 2:13-16
8. Eph 5:22-23
9. Eph 5:21
10. 1 Pet 3:7
11. Mark 16:17-18
12. Rom 13
13. Eph 5:28-29
14. 1 Tim 5:8
15. Eph 6:4
16. Gen 1:27, 5:2
17. Exod 15:3
18. Matt 23:37; Luke 3:34
19. Deut 32:11 KJV
20. Isa 66:13
21. Matt 5:14
22. 1 Cor 12:4-11
23. 2 Cor 3:18

23. UNITE

1. Prov 14:1
2. Eph 5:21
3. Mal 2:13-16
4. Luke 6:32-36
5. Mal 2:11
6. Mal 2:16
7. 1 John 4:7-8

24. COLLABORATE

1. Rev 19:10
2. Rev 19:7
3. Rom 8:29
4. Col 1:27
5. 1 Cor 12
6. Matt 20:28

25. CHANGE THE WORLD

1. Luke 15:31
2. Matt 7:7
3. Prov 18:19
4. 1 Pet 2:17
5. Eph 4:11-16
6. Mal 4:6; Luke 1:17
7. Eph 1:5
8. Matt 3:17
9. Acts 2:46
10. Luke 15:22-31
11. Ps 23:5
12. Matt 26:17-30
13. Rev 19:6-9
14. Acts 2:42
15. Acts 2:42-47
16. 1 Pet 5:5

26. LEAVE A LEGACY

1. Phil 1:21
2. John 12:24
3. Luke 16:10
4. Matt 5:21, 23
5. Acts 2:17
6. John 7:38
7. John 15:5
8. Mal 3:10
9. Matt 13:23
10. Esth 8-9
11. 1 Cor 7:10-17
12. Heb 13:2-3
13. Isa 9:7
14. John 15:1-8
15. 2 Cor 10:5
16. Rom 1:18-32
17. Phil 1:6
18. John 15:1-8
19. 1 Corinthians 2:9
20. Eccl 7:8

CONCLUSION

21. 2 Cor 3:18
22. Rom 8:18-23

1. Prov 18:22
2. Ps 139:14
3. Prov 5
4. Prov 11:22
5. 1 Cor 7
6. 1 Tim 5:8
7. Mark 10:9
8. Gen 3
9. Gen 3:13
10. Eph 6:12
11. Matt 14:14
12. Ps 127:3-5
13. Gen 2:24
14. Gal 5:22
15. John 4:10, 7:37-39
16. Matt 6:11; John 6:35, 6:51
17. Rom 1:18-32
18. Rom 1:20-28
19. Gen 1:27
20. Rom 1:26-27
21. Prov 18:22
22. 1 Tim 2:14
23. 1 Tim 2:14
24. Gen 3:6
25. Gen 2:15-18
26. Luke 18:1-8
27. 1 Cor 14:34-35
28. Acts 17:22-31
29. Mal 2:10-15
30. 2 Cor 11:14
31. Eph 5:22-32
32. Gen 3:15
33. Rom 5:8
34. 1 John 4:19
35. Hag 2:7
36. Esth 4:14
37. Esth 5:2

38. Prov 8:1-15
39. Isa 54:1
40. 2 Cor 3:17
41. Deut 30:19
42. Prov 31:25
43. Prov 31:30